THE REALM
of OSIRIS

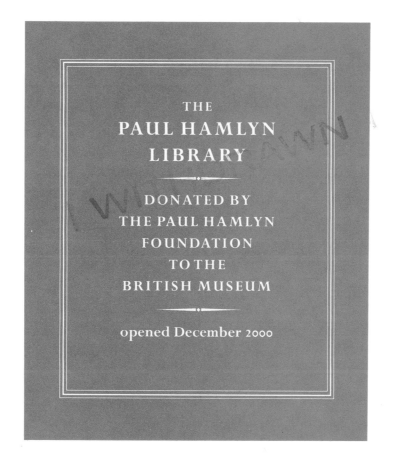

THE REALM *of* OSIRIS

Mummies, Coffins, and Ancient Egyptian Funerary Art in the Michael C. Carlos Museum

EDITED BY

PETER LACOVARA AND BETSY TEASLEY TROPE

Michael C. Carlos Museum
Emory University
Atlanta 2001

Copyright © 2001 Michael C. Carlos Museum

ISBN 1-928917-04-6

Designed by Times 3, Atlanta
Production editor: Alexa Selph

Printed in the United States of America by Williams Printing Company, Atlanta

Photographic credits:

All catalogue entry photographs are by Peter Harholdt or Michael McKelvey.

All other photographs are from the archives of the Michael C. Carlos Museum.

All line drawings are by Ande Cook.

COVER DETAIL:
Lid of the Coffin of Tanakhtnettahat
(cat. no. 38)
Dynasty 21, 1075–945 BC
Wood, pigment
Coffin: L. 181.5 cm; w. 52 cm; d. 55.5 cm
1999.1.17 B
Charlotte Lichirie Collection of Egyptian Art

To the citizens of Georgia

whose spontaneous outpouring of support

made this project possible

Contents

Foreword and Acknowledgments

THE FUNERARY ART OF ANCIENT EGYPT has formed part of the collection at Emory University since 1920, when Dr. William A. Shelton of Emory's School of Theology traveled to Egypt and the Near East to purchase antiquities that would inform students about the cultural milieu of the lands of the Bible. He brought back wrapped mummies, painted coffins, and many other artifacts that were then, as they are now, among the best-loved material on display. These objects remained at the core of the collection during the decades of faithful stewardship of the Emory University Museum by Dr. Woolford B. Baker, who served as curator and then director. During his tenure the Museum became widely known in Atlanta as "the mummy museum," and many who grew up in town still have fond memories of talking with Dr. Baker about the collection. The Museum began to refine and focus its mission in the 1970s, and in 1984 it was renamed the Emory University Museum of Art and Archaeology, with the Egyptian material serving as a focal point for the permanent collection. In 1993 the Museum was renamed the Michael C. Carlos Museum, honoring its greatest benefactor, Michael C. Carlos, whose generosity made possible an expansion to nearly triple the size of the previous space.

In 1988, Emory hired its first Egyptologist, Dr. Gay Robins. Professor Robins, a scholar of wide renown, assisted the Museum as its Faculty Curator of ancient Egyptian art, and it was her hand that shaped the Egyptian galleries in the current Museum facilities. When Peter Lacovara, himself a distinguished Egyptologist, joined the Museum's staff in 1998 as its first full-time Curator of Ancient Art, the pace of activity quickened remarkably. His contacts in the museum community worldwide were well aware of his passion to see the Carlos Museum's Egyptian holdings grow. Through one of his colleagues in Canada he learned that an extraordinary Egyptian collection, maintained since the nineteenth century by the small, privately owned Niagara Falls Museum, would soon become available on the international market. In short order, Thérèse O'Gorman, the Museum's conservator, joined Dr. Lacovara in inspecting the collection and expressing support for its potential acquisition.

In early 1999, the Museum's Board of Directors, led by its Chairman, James B. Miller, Jr., enthusiastically endorsed the idea, and significant pledges of support began to come in. There was reason to worry, however, for the Niagara Falls material was being offered to other institutions around the globe. When the story of the Museum's effort to acquire the collection appeared on the front page of the *Atlanta Journal-Constitution*, however, the citizens of Atlanta responded in a most remarkable way. Contributions poured in from foundations and individuals of all types, including classes of school-children and those who had never visited the Carlos Museum before but wanted this prize for their city. Within a week, over three hundred donors had responded with gifts ranging from $10 to $1 million. The deed was done. In May 1999, the collection left for its new home.

The Museum's staff and Board shared a commitment to make this new material accessible as soon as possible to the citizens who had banded together to purchase it. Fall 2001 was agreed upon as a target date, and work began immediately.

This acquisition has given Atlanta a collection of Egyptian funerary art rivaled by only a handful of cities in the country and none in the South. As the Museum's expanded conservation staff raced to clean, stabilize, and conserve all the material that had arrived from Niagara Falls, the curatorial department labored tirelessly, consulting colleagues from around the world, to research it. The exhibition design department worked closely with the Museum's architect, Michael Graves, and his office to create beautiful new galleries of Egyptian, Nubian, and Near Eastern Art in renovated space to house the Egyptian collections. News media from around the globe took an interest in the collection. With the new, extraordinary strength in Egyptian funerary material and beautiful new galleries to house it all, it was clear that the Museum should produce the present publication to document the collection.

Any endeavor of such scope requires the work of an extraordinary number of people and organizations. We are deeply grateful to all of them; had any one of them faltered, the enterprise might well have come to a halt. No member of the Museum's staff was left untouched by the project, and each of them responded with his or her customary (but otherwise extraordinary) professionalism, dedication, intelligence, and good temper.

First and foremost, it is to Peter Lacovara, the Carlos Museum's Curator of Ancient Egyptian, Nubian, and Near Eastern Art, that we owe the greatest debt of gratitude. His vision, experience, network of contacts, and endless hours of hard work have made this project possible. Betsy Teasley Trope, Assistant Curator for the Permanent Collection and an Egyptologist herself, labored with the same dedication, and the project could not have been brought to fruition without her. Monique Brouillet Seefried, Adjunct Curator of Ancient Near Eastern Art, has long selflessly promoted the work of the Museum both internally and externally. Again in this instance, she made contributions of inestimable value. Piper Phillips, Curatorial Assistant, Brandon Foster, a graduate student and Andrew W. Mellon Foundation intern, and Jennifer Gates all lent their considerable skills to the project. Graduate students Laura Brannen and Jane Rehl have been invaluable in preparing the labels for the new galleries.

Thérèse O'Gorman, the Museum's Conservator, expertly supervised the expansion of her laboratory facilities and staff to accommodate the challenging schedule of work. She was joined in the lab by a superb team, including Renée Stein, Assistant Conservator, and contract conservators Katherine Singley and Alexandra Klingelhofer, all of whom did first-class work in record time. Ron Harvey, an experienced conservator from Maine, assisted in the packing of material in Canada and then came to Atlanta for several extended visits to work further with it. Margaret LeVeque, a textile conservator who specializes in the treatment of the wrappings of mummified remains, did a remarkable job of dealing with materials that had been roughly treated for decades. Conor McMahon, originally an undergraduate student in Ms. O'Gorman's class, moved on through an internship, an Andrew W. Mellon Foundation internship, and part-time employment in the conservation lab, where he became indispensable. Also, for three months, the Museum had the good fortune to have an Egyptian conservator, Abd El-Rahman Mohammed El-Serogy, participate in the work, thanks to a grant from the American Research Center in Egypt, which, in the wake of the acquisition, moved its American headquarters to the Emory campus. Volunteers Joan Sammons-Hodges and Eleanor Ridley assisted in the Parsons Conservation Laboratory with exemplary diligence, and Gail Walter and Bennie McGinley lent their skills in beadworking to the restoration of ancient jewelry. Carol Hopkins masterfully organized the conservation records and temporary storage for objects.

At the Museum, it is also necessary to acknowledge the great good work of Nancy Roberts, Coordinator of Exhibition Design, who carried her responsibilities forward with her customary superb taste and calm despite the challenges. Among her staff, all of whom performed small miracles on a regular basis, Karen Chance, Stephen Bodnar, Deborah Monroy, Chris Sancomb, and Mike Jensen are to be particularly commended. Without Stephen Bodnar's leadership, the coffins would never have left Niagara Falls. Several volunteers have generously assisted the department in preparing the fabric covering for risers and display case panels: our sincere thanks go to Bev Center, Lindsay Marshall, Julia McBride, Bennie McGinley, Joan Sammons-Hodges, Gail Walter, and Nancy Wiesner for their help in this area.

In the Registrar's Office, three Registrars in succession, Stacey Savatsky, Maureen Morrisette, and Todd Lamkin, all performed with extraordinary valor through endless complications. Melody James, Assistant Registrar, lent her many talents to this project as well, including serving as Acting Registrar when she had to bear the responsibilities of the department alone, transporting mummies to Emory University Hospital and deftly orchestrating all the complex photography the project required.

The Registrar's Office coordinated the many loans and gifts of objects to the reinstallation of the galleries. We are deeply grateful to Alan Safani, Jerome Eisenberg, Don Snyder, Yvonne Markowitz, Jean-Louis Domercq, Meg Robbins, John Silva, Judy and Billy Cottle, Drs. Ann and Robert Walzer, and Sally and Jim Morgens for their generous gifts of works of art and resources to assist the Museum in purchasing works that enhance the new installation. We are also indebted to the lenders of objects, including Tom Scapillato, Paul Mooney, Deidre Abrams, Jerome Eisenberg, Jonathan Rosen, Bob Brier, Gay Robins, Jasper Gaunt, Betsy Teasley Trope, Tom Swope, and, in particular, Lewis M. Dubroff and his family, for sharing so many wonderful treasures with us.

The new galleries will also attest to the success of the Museum Loan Network, a program funded by the John S. and James L. Knight Foundation and the Pew Charitable Trust. Based at the Massachusetts Institute of Technology and administered through MIT's Office of the Arts, the program was developed in 1995 to promote and foster collection-sharing of art objects on a long-term basis among museums in the United States. Thanks to this program, the rich collections of the Cleveland Museum of Art, the Harvard Semitic Museum, the Harvard Peabody Museum, the Peabody Essex Museum, and the Worcester Art Museum will find a fresh audience in Atlanta and enhance our new galleries. Additional loans were also provided by the Museum of Fine Arts, Boston. These will complement loan objects already provided through the munificence of the Metropolitan Museum of Art, the Oriental Institute of the University of Chicago, and the Royal Ontario Museum.

Elizabeth Hornor, Director of Educational Programs, and her colleagues Julie Green, Manager of School Programs, and Bruce Raper, Manager of Youth and Family Programs, created an extraordinary array of educational programming to accompany the opening of the new galleries. Although she joined the staff only months before the opening of the new galleries, Lucie André was essential in her role as the Museum's Director of Development and External Affairs, as was Alicia Franck, Emory's Associate Vice President for Development. Gail Habif, Carrie Nellis, Jay Cuasay, and Leigh Burns worked diligently to respond to the extraordinary needs for member, visitor, and donor services. The Museum's Coordinators of Marketing and Public Relations, first Joy Bell and then Allison Germaneso Dixon, orchestrated responses to the endless inquiries from the media with great aplomb. Diann Crider worked to assist Ms. Bell and also to coordinate all of the work with the Emory University Hospital and the DNA researchers. Later on, Lindsay Marshall, a Museum docent and volunteer, ably took on this role.

Complex budget matters were handled with great skill by successive Managers of Personnel and Budget, Jennifer Gossett and Darlene Hayes. Mark Burell, Manager of the Museum Bookshop, ably coped with heavy demand for all things Egyptian, assisted by Sasha Buzzetta and Jonathan Green. In the director's office, Joyce Daniels maintained her characteristic good humor and level head, keeping things organized despite the pressures. Richard Endress and, after his retirement, Bernard Potts, Managers of Operations, kept things running smoothly behind the scenes during the renovation of the new galleries. Finally, enormous thanks must be extended to Catherine Howett Smith, the Museum's Associate Director and Director of Academic Services. Her involvement embraced nearly every aspect of the project, and the Museum relied on her good sense, superior management skills, and organizational abilities to keep things on track during a very hectic period in the Museum's history.

Colleagues from around the world assisted the Museum's staff in this project. Among the most important were Joyce Haynes, Yvonne Markowitz, Sheila Shear, Larry Berman, and Denise Doxey of the Museum of Fine Arts, Boston; John Taylor of the British Museum; mummy experts Bob Brier, James Harris, and Salima Ikram; Dorothea Arnold, Marsha Hill, Diana Craig Patch, and Catherine Roehrig of the Metropolitan Museum of Art; and Sue D'Auria, formerly of the MFA, Boston, and now working for the Huntington Museum of Art in West Virginia. Wilma Wetterstrom of Harvard University's Botanical Museum kindly provided identifications of the ancient plant materials in the collection.

From the start, Emory University Hospital offered unstinting assistance as we sought information about the nine mummies that came to Atlanta in 1999. The hospital employees who participated in conducting CT-scans, X-rays, and endoscopic testing number in the dozens, but foremost among them we owe thanks to Kaye Barefield, M.D.; Kathy Boone, R.T.; Ben George, R.T.; Steve Goldschmid, M.D.; Rita Harden, R.N.; Heidi Hoffman, M.D.; Martha Howard, librarian and media specialist; Beverly Markott, R.N.; Eric Mutz, M.D.; Mary Kaye O'Brien, R.T.; Sharon Sassar, R.T.; Shanti Sitaraman, M.D.; William E. Torres, M.D.; Dianne Williams, R.N.; and Shirley Wray. Dr. Hoffman, along with Sue D'Auria, also wrote the essay in this catalogue on mummies and modern medical imaging. Martin Hunsinger, a General Electric technician, generously made himself available to run the equipment for every CT-scanning session. We are also grateful to Mike McCarthy, of Olympus.

Dr. Douglas Wallace, one of the world's most distinguished genetic researchers, his postdoctoral students Jeff Lell and Dan Mishmar, and others on his team at Emory spent long hours working in a state-of-the-art facility to consider the genetic evidence provided by the mummies, including the one that, it has been suggested, could be that of the pharaoh Ramesses I. Further investigation of that possibility is ongoing.

None of this important work would have been possible if it had not been for the enormously generous financial support of many individuals, foundations, companies, and organizations. Those who supported the effort recognized the importance of this opportunity for the Carlos Museum, for Emory University, for Atlanta, and for the region. First and foremost among them is the Chairman of the Museum's Board of Directors, James B. Miller, Jr., who, with his wife, Karina, pledged $1 million to the effort to acquire the collection from Niagara Falls, so convinced were they that this was a defining moment in the history of the Museum. It was their wish that the new collection would bear the name of Mrs. Miller's mother, Charlotte Lichirie, to honor her generosity and her lifelong interest in Egypt, and thus it is now known as the Charlotte Lichirie Collection of Egyptian Art.

Other donors too deserve special recognition. The Forward Arts Foundation, an organization that has quietly helped several key arts organizations in the Atlanta area for over thirty years, chose to dedicate one of its largest gifts, $250,000, to the acquisition. Thanks are due particularly to Betty Edge, then the President of Forward Arts, for her efforts to get a decision with lightning speed. The newly formed John Goddard Foundation made its first gift to the acquisition. The Evergreen Foundation also gave generously, as did Michael C. Carlos, one of his many acts of benevolence toward the Museum over the years; his gift was the one that allowed the Museum to complete the fund-raising effort for the Lichirie Collection. Anne Cox Chambers, Gary and Ruth Rollins, and Mary Rose Taylor were also extremely generous in supporting the acquisition. A list of all those who participated in this remarkable initiative follows this Foreword.

Even these gifts would not have allowed the Museum to move forward if Emory University, under the leadership of President William Chace and its Board of Trustees, had not agreed to purchase the collection for the Museum on the strength of signed, multi-year pledges of support. Emory has offered consistent and generous partnership to the Museum over the years, and the support of the administration in this instance was absolutely critical to the effort's success.

After the acquisition was certain, more funding needed to be obtained to cover the substantial costs of research, conservation, and installation in new galleries. To this effort, no one made a more important contribution than Jan Bennett, the chair of the Museum's gala, Veneralia, in 2001. "A Night on the Nile" was an enormous success, and all the proceeds were invested in the reinstallation. To Jan, Heather Howard of Destination South, and all the volunteers who worked so hard to make the evening a success, we extend the warmest thanks.

The James M. Cox, Jr. Foundation, which has done much to preserve Atlanta's most important treasures for all its citizens, recognized the importance of conserving the works in the new collection with a remarkable gift of $250,000. An anonymous donor also recognized the importance of the work going on at the Museum and made a significant gift in honor of former Coca-Cola executive and beloved Museum Board member Sam Ayoub. Others followed suit. The Rich Foundation contributed to the cost of creating the handsome new gallery spaces for the collection despite its other major commitments at Emory University. The National Endowment for the Arts, a federal agency, supported the educational programming accompanying the new installation. In addition, the Georgia Council for the Arts provided an extraordinary grant, for which we were tremendously grateful.

We are also grateful to the many members of the media who took an interest in the story. First, we must thank Catherine Fox, the visual arts reporter for the *Atlanta Journal-Constitution,* and her editors at the newspaper. Her stories on the Museum's attempt to acquire the Lichirie Collection gave life to the communitywide effort. WSB-TV also followed the story closely, producing two television documentaries of the highest quality. At WSB, I would like to thank John Pruitt, the host of the specials; Leona Nascimento, the videographer who stayed with the project from the first; and writer-producers Chris Cantergianni and C. B. Hackworth. Further thanks are owed to Art Rogers and Ray Carter, executive producers; John Reed, post-production editor; Jane Cole, associate producer; Jim Dixon and Alex Houvouras, graphic artists; Dave Darling and Scott Huffman, photographers; and Jeff Geesen, audio. Also, I want to extend warm thanks to Jonathan Wickham, an independent producer, and his colleagues for their boundless enthusiasm and curiosity as they developed a program for the PBS series *Nova.*

Finally, I must thank Robert Evans of Times 3, who, as usual, produced a gorgeous book in very little time with his usual good cheer and flawless taste, and Alexa Selph, a gifted editor as well as a Museum docent, who edited the catalogue in record time. Peter Harholdt and Michael McKelvey provided the beautiful photographs that grace this volume. Ande Cook skillfully drafted the line drawings that enhance both the catalogue and the interpretive materials for the installation.

We are delighted to present this publication, introducing one of the most important and visible parts of the Michael C. Carlos Museum's collection, to audiences in Atlanta and around the world who care deeply about the intriguing funerary arts of ancient Egypt. We hope that it will serve as a companion to many visits to the galleries, as well as an important work of scholarship in its own right.

ANTHONY HIRSCHEL
Director
Michael C. Carlos Museum

Further Acknowledgments

The Michael C. Carlos Museum gratefully acknowledges the following donors who claimed the Charlotte Lichirie Collection of Egyptian Art for Atlanta. Their contributions, ranging from $10 to a remarkable $1 million, were sent or pledged in less than a month's time in early 1999. Each gift was tremendously meaningful.

In addition to those listed here, thanks go to the Museum members, volunteers, friends, and benefactors whose steadfast support for all the Museum's endeavors will enable the Carlos Museum to care for the Collection, allowing its presence to resonate for generations.

Mr. & Mrs. Charles Ackerman
Acrylic Acumen
Virginia Adair
Douglas L. Allen
Elkin Alston
Judy Andrews
Arbor Montessori School
Betty Litsey's class of
	Arbor Montessori School
Irene C. Aronin
Arthur Andersen Foundation
Jean Astrop
William Atkinson
Mark & Anne Austin
William & Carolyn Avery
In honor of Sam Ayoub
Merrily Baird
Becky Baldwin
Eugene Bales, Jr.
Rebecca & Randale Bankston
Roger & Wanda Bankston
Thomas & Susan Barfield
Marcy Bass
Jimmy & Carolyn Beasley
BellSouth
Beloit Properties
Gwendolyn Bergen
Ginger Beverly
Big Buddy Farm
Octavia Riley Birnie
Dr. & Mrs. Donald Block
Tim & Sylvia Bolduan
Paungthip Boonperm-Weniger
C. William & Eda Boroughs
Robert G. Boroughs
Lynn Boyd
Clairose Brannen
Elinor & William Breman Fund
Kathryn & Billy Bridges
Katherine, Patty, Becky, & Gail Brooks
Patricia E. Brooks
Rebecca S. Brooks
The Mary Brown Fund of Atlanta
Albert & Joyce Buggs
Cathy Callaway

Mr. & Mrs. Michael C. Carlos
Melissa Carman
William & Jane Carney
Arvilla Carpenter
Mr. & Mrs. James E. Carter
John B. Carter, Jr.
Bev Center
JoAn & Bill Chace
The Honorable Anne Cox Chambers
Chamblee High School Class of 2001
Miyoko Chang
Bill & Carolyn Childers
Rebecca Chopp
Allen & Claudia Clark
The Coca-Cola Company
A Collector's Choice
Dr. & Mrs. John T. Cobb
Mary Condo
Terry & Ginny Connelly
State Representative Sharon Cooper
Richard Corbin
Craig & Vartorella International
	Marketing
Mimi Cromwell
Peter Dakutis
Stephen & Margaret Dana
Katherine Dannenberg
Jenny Day
James & Linda Debenedictis
Dr. & Mrs. Brown Dennis
Kenneth & Barbara Disque
Kathy & Rogers Dixson
Bridget Dobson
Paul S. Dominey
Barbara Downing
Mary Catherine Dudley
Gary Duesterberg & Adora Ku
Catherine Dukehart
Tom Eddins, Jr.
Mike & Stephanie Edmonds
Ralph M. Edmonds
Eleven Eleven Fund/Floyd W. McRae
Emory University
Hans & Marie Ernst
Anne Estes

Ethical Advertising
Roy & Franci Ethridge
The Evergreen Foundation
Martha & James Fagan
Ken Falck
Doyle Faler
Federal National Mortgage
Federated Department Stores, Inc.
Jeanne Ferst
Carol Fetters
Scott Fisher & Marcy Bass
Patrick Flinn & Karen Hegtvedt
Diane Foley
James A. Ford
The Forward Arts Foundation
Julia Foster & Family
Edgar & Anne Fowlkes
William Fox
Steve Fraser
Billy & Elisa Frye
William Funk & Gayle Gellerstedt
Sarah B. Gable
William & Irmgard Gimby
Mrs. J. R. Gladden
Sally & Joe Gladden
Lyndel Gliedman
The John N. Goddard Foundation
James Goodrum
Mark Gould
Lee Graham III
Lelia J. Graham
John G. Grant
Greater Atlanta Archaeological Society
Leslie Claire Green
Troy & Jan Green
Sharon Greene
David J. Grindle
Gail & Michael Habif
Maryam Haddad
Jo Ann Haden-Miller
Betz Halloran
Alice Ann Hamilton
Hance Hamilton
Laura Hardman
A. Stevens Harris

Susan P. Hasbrouck
Norman A. Hartman, Jr., &
    Barbara L. Hartman
Donald & Katherine Hatcher
Alexander Hawes
Craig & Mary Hayes
Rich & Cathy Hayes
John Hays & Anna Mershon
Karen A. Hegtvedt
Helen Jancik Unlimited
Mr. & Mrs. George R. Hemenway
George Hemenway, Jr.
Cynthia Hewett
Edwin Heyer
Dr. & Mrs. Benjamin Hill
D. W. Hindsman
Alex Hitz, Jr.
James A. Hoeper
Thomas M. Holder
Charles E. Hoover
Harriet Hoskyns-Abrahall
Mrs. William E. Huger, Jr.
Barbara Hull
Betty & Billy Hulse
Laura Hunter
IBM Corporation Foundation
Roland & Marguerite Ingram
Jack & Jill of America
Mrs. Ellen Pearson's Kindergarten Class,
    Jackson Elementary
Helen & Jim Jancik
Charlotte Johnson
Baxter P. Jones
Douglas & Judy Jones
Mr. & Mrs. Frank C. Jones
Gary & Celeste Katz
Cherie Kidd
Richard & Martha Kiefer
Henrietta Kilpatrick
Fanny King
Don Knight
Thomas & Jo Koch
Margie Koenig
James & Mary Koger
Julian & Annette Kolby

Arnold & Joan Kurth
Carol Lander
Jeff Langenderfer & Susan Hasbrouck
Robert & Ruth Lee
John David & Pat Lindholm
Guy Edward Lites III
David Llewellyn
Barbara Loar
Lucent Technologies Foundation
Lawrence & Ruth Mandt
Michael & Anita Mann
Barbara Manning
The Massey Charitable Trust
Adair R. Massey
Luis Maza
Mary Ben McDorman
Lee McEachern
Patton & Bennie McGinley
Greg & Audrey McMenamy
Jim McNamara
James Messenger
Mike Meyer
James B. and Karina Miller
Dorothy H. Miller
Patricia T. Miller
Sharon Ruth Mitchell
Laura Moore
Ted & Mary N. Moore/
    Chrysalis Foundation
Morgens West Foundation
Christopher Morter
Stanley & Jane Mulaik
Hannah Murray
Museums & Galleries Atlanta
Edie Murphree
Serge P. Neprash
Steve & Peggy Newfield
New World Communications, Inc.
Michelle & Bertil Nordin
North American Van Lines
Walter A. Ogle & Raymond Cottingham
Boone and Mollie-Emma O'Neil
George A. & Kelley P. Ort
John & Marilyn Pahr
Elizabeth Painter

Albert Parker
Penny Parker
Marguerite Paul
Pattillo Family Foundation
John F. Pensec
Melvin & Marilyn Perling
Sigfred Peterson
Elizabeth Phelan
Photovoltaic Insider's Report
Pitch & Putt Liquor Store
Pittulloch Foundation
Catherine Porter
Dr. Jerry Dean Porter
B.M. Potlock
Susan & Dick Plunkett
Janette B. Pratt
Brenda & Walton Rawls
Emily Redwine
George Redwine
Wendell & Mary Reilly
Beverlie Reilman
Carl Renfroe
Regine Reynolds-Cornell
Clayton & Sally Rich
Sarah P. Rich
Dr. & Mrs. Henry C. Ricks, Jr.
Clancy & Eleanor Ridley
Dr. & Mrs. James Riggans
Mary Robbins
Gay Robins
Robinson Family Foundation
Amy J. Robinson
Doris Robinson
Radine Robinson
Deidre Thompson Roche
Ruthie & Gary Rollins
Jane Rooney
William & Carlotta Rosenthal
Danny & Queenie Ross
Mark & Mary Rusch
Joan Sammons
Richard & Leanna Sandefur
The Scarborough Family
Carla Schissel
Jeffrey & Elizabeth Schulte

Daniel Schumm
Ira & Janet Schwartz
Olivia & Burton Scott
Monique Seefried
Senoia Variety Club
Dr. & Mrs. George Sessions
Shepherd Foundation
Margaret Duvall Shufeldt
Karen & James Sibley
Karen Mariea Sibley
Vee Simmons
Gary & Amy Simons
Marjory Simpkins
Kwai Sing & Miyoko Chang
Gail B. Smith
Hugh & June Smith
William Snellings
Donald Snyder
Peter & Lindsey Sones
Anne Spratlin
Juliet Stahl
Raymond & Catherine Stainback, Jr.
Dr. & Mrs. David Stacy
Mary Helen Stakely
Michael & Lynda Stargel
Lois Starr
Judy & Jim Stevens
Mary E. Stevens
Laura Stock
SunTrust Bank, Atlanta Foundation
David Tate
Anne Taustin
Judith & Mark Taylor
Mary Rose Taylor
John Temple
Mrs. Romulus H. Thompson
Isabel D. Thomson
Kate & Elwyn Tomlinson
Linda Trickey
Turner Foundation, Inc.
Joyce Turner
Variety Club
Cristina Vasconez
Mrs. James H. Vason
Patty Vick

Viva Foundation
James L. Wagstaff
John A. Wallace
William & Cecile Waronker
Bernice Weinstein
Howard & Joan Weinstein
Helen & Alvin Weeks Foundation
Tom & Kathy Weller
West Georgia College
    Anthropology Society
Nina & Frances West
Mrs. Richard Wheeler & Gus Wheeler
George & Joan White
John A. White, Jr.
Raymond White, Sr.
James Whitfield
Paul & Nancy Wiesner
Mr. & Mrs. Larry C. Williams
Loraine & Tom Williams
Thomas L. Williams
Mary F. Wilmer
Mike & SuSu Wimberley
Sarah Morgan Wingfield
Scott & Kimberly Withrow
Caroline Woodall
David Woodbury
Chevin Woodruff
Woodward Academy Lower School
    6th Grade
Barry & Jennifer Yaffe
Sidney H. Yarbrough III
Daniel & Mary Young
Margaret Zolliker, M.D.

This nineteenth-century photograph shows a merchant selling mummies on a street corner in Egypt. Local vendors supplied tourists with mummies and coffins—both real and fake—to satisfy the Victorian fascination with these ancient relics. Agents for the Niagara Falls Museum would have negotiated with entrepreneurs like these to form their collection, now part of the holdings of the Michael C. Carlos Museum.

Mummy Seller
Félix Bonfils
French (1831–1885)
Albumen print, 1883
Photo courtesy of William Knight Zewadski.

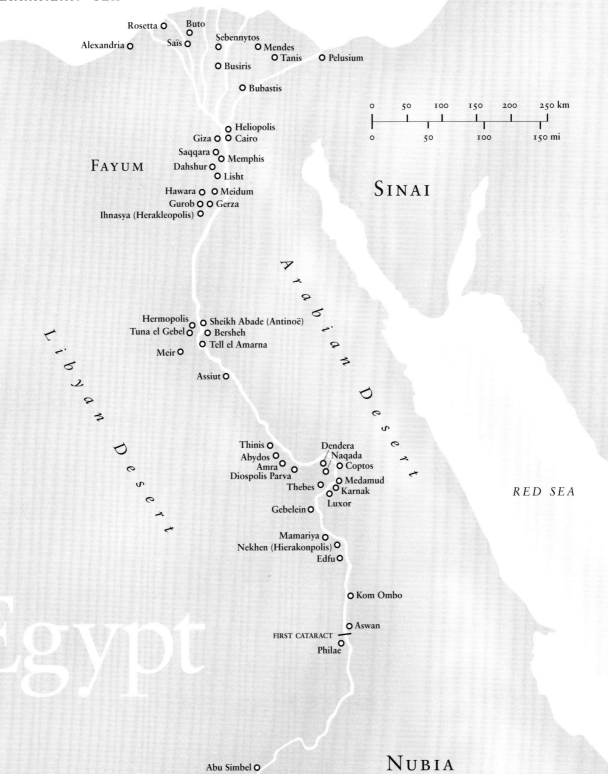

MEDITERRANEAN SEA

Rosetta ○   Buto ○
Alexandria ○   Saïs ○   Sebennytos ○
                                    ○ Mendes
                                    ■ Tanis   ● Pelusium
            ○ Busiris

            ○ Bubastis

                        ○ Heliopolis
        Giza ○ ○ Cairo
FAYUM   Saqqara ○ ○ Memphis
        Dahshur ○
                ○ Lisht
    Hawara ○ ○ Meidum
    Gurob ○ ○ Gerza
Ihnasya (Herakleopolis) ○

SINAI

0   50   100   150   200   250 km
0   50   100   150 mi

Libyan Desert

Arabian Desert

Hermopolis ○ ○ Sheikh Abade (Antinoë)
Tuna el Gebel ○ ○ Bersheh
    Meir ○ ○ Tell el Amarna

        ○ Assiut

RED SEA

Thinis ○   Dendera
Abydos ○   ○ Naqada
    Amra ○   ○ Coptos
Diospolis Parva   ○ Medamud
    Thebes ○ ○ Karnak
        ○ Luxor
Gebelein ○

    Mamariya ○
Nekhen (Hierakonpolis) ○
        Edfu ○

            ○ Kom Ombo

                ○ Aswan
FIRST CATARACT ╱
        Philae ●

Egypt

Abu Simbel ○
    Faras ○

NUBIA

╱ SECOND CATARACT

Chronology of Egyptian History

This chronology follows that found in William J. Murnane, "The History of Ancient Egypt," in *Civilizations of the Ancient Near East*, edited by Jack M. Sasson et al. (New York, 1995), 712–14.

PREDYNASTIC PERIOD
(UPPER EGYPT)

Badarian *4800–4200 BC*
Naqada I (Amratian) *4200–3700 BC*
Naqada II (Gerzean) *3700–3250 BC*
Naqada III (Late Gerzean–Dynasty 0) *3250–3100 BC*

ARCHAIC PERIOD

Dynasty 1 *3100–2907 BC*
Dynasty 2 *2907–2755 BC*
Dynasty 3 *2755–2625 BC*
   Djoser (Netjerikhet) *2687–2667 BC*

OLD KINGDOM
   2625–2130 BC

Dynasty 4 *2625–2500 BC*
   Sneferu *2625–2585 BC*
   Khufu (Cheops) *2585–2560 BC*
   Khafre (Chephren) *2555–2532 BC*
   Menkaure (Mycerinus) *2532–2510 BC*
Dynasty 5 *2500–2350 BC*
   Unas *2371–2350 BC*
Dynasty 6 *2350–2170 BC*
   Pepy I *2338–2298 BC*
   Pepy II *2288–2224/2194 BC*
Dynasties 7/8 *2170–2130 BC*

FIRST INTERMEDIATE PERIOD
   2130–1980 BC

Dynasties 9/10 (Herakleopolitan) *2130–1980 BC*
Dynasty 11 (Theban) *2081–1938 BC*

MIDDLE KINGDOM
   1980–1630 BC

Dynasty 11 *2008–1957 BC*
   Nebhepetre Montuhotep II *2008–1957 BC*
   Sankhkare Montuhotep III *1957–1945 BC*
   Nebtawyre Montuhotep IV *1945–1938 BC*
Dynasty 12 *1938–1759 BC*
   Amenemhet I *1938–1909 BC*
   Sesostris I *1919–1875 BC*
   Amenemhet II *1876–1842 BC*
   Sesostris II *1844–1837 BC*
   Sesostris III *1836–1818 BC*
   Amenemhet III *1818–1772 BC*
Dynasty 13 *1759–after 1630 BC*
Dynasty 14 (contemporaneous with later Dynasty 13)

SECOND INTERMEDIATE PERIOD
   1630–1539/23 BC

Dynasty 15 (Hyksos) *1630–1523 BC*
Dynasty 16 (contemporaneous with D. 15) *1630–1523 BC*
Dynasty 17 (Theban) *1630–1539 BC*
   Seqenenre Tao *?–1543? BC*
   Kamose *1543?–1539 BC*

NEW KINGDOM
   1539–1075 BC

Dynasty 18 *1539–1292 BC*
   Hatshepsut *1478/72–1458 BC*
   Thutmose III *1479–1425 BC*
   Amenhotep II *1426–1400 BC*
   Thutmose IV *1400–1390 BC*
   Amenhotep III *1390–1353 BC*
   Amenhotep IV (Akhenaten) *1353–1336 BC*
   Tutankhamen *1332–1322 BC*
Dynasty 19 (Ramesside) *1292–1190 BC*
   Ramesses I *1292–1290 BC*
   Seti I *1290–1279 BC*
   Ramesses II *1279–1213 BC*
Dynasty 20 (Ramesside) *1190–1075 BC*

THIRD INTERMEDIATE PERIOD
1075–656 BC

Dynasty 21 (Tanite) *1075–945 BC*

Dynasty 22 (Bubastite) *945–712 BC*

  Shoshenq I *945–924 BC*

  Osorkon II *874–835/30 BC*

Dynasty 23 *838–712 BC*

Dynasty 24 (Saite) *727–712 BC*

  Tefnakht *727–719 BC*

Dynasty 25 (in Egypt) *760–656 BC*

  Kashta *760–747 BC*

  Piye *747–716 BC*

  Shabaka *716–702 BC*

  Shebitku *702–690 BC*

  Taharqa *690–664 BC*

  Tantamani *664–656 BC*

Dynasty 25 (continuing in Nubia)
  653–ca. 300 BC

  Senkamanisken *643–623 BC*

  Anlamani *623–593 BC*

  Aspelta *593–568 BC*

LATE PERIOD
664–332 BC

Dynasty 26 (Saite) *664–525 BC*

  Psamtek I *664–610 BC*

  Psamtek II *595–589 BC*

  Apries *589–570 BC*

  Amasis *570–526 BC*

Dynasty 27 (First Persian Period)
  525–404 BC

  Cambyses *525–522 BC*

  Darius I *521–486 BC*

  Xerxes I *485–465 BC*

Dynasty 28 *404–399 BC*

Dynasty 29 (Mendes) *399–380 BC*

Dynasty 30 (Sebennytos) *381–343 BC*

  Nectanebo I *381–362 BC*

  Nectanebo II (last native king)
    362–343 BC

Persian Reconquest
  343–332 BC

GRAECO-ROMAN PERIOD
332 BC–AD 642

Macedonian Dynasty *332–305 BC*

  Alexander *332–323 BC*

  Philip III Arrhidaeus *323–305 BC*

Ptolemaic Dynasty *305–30BC*

  Ptolemy I Soter *305–282 BC*

  Cleopatra VII Philopator *51–30 BC*

Roman, later Byzantine, Empire
  30 BC–AD 642

  Augustus *30 BC–AD 14 BC*

  Tiberius *AD 14–37*

  Claudius *AD 41–54*

  Domitian *AD 81–96*

  Trajan *AD 98–117*

  Decius *AD 249–251*

COPTIC PERIOD
Late 2nd century AD–AD 642

ARAB CONQUEST
AD 642

An interior view of the Niagara Falls Museum, probably taken during the nineteenth century.

Emory and Egypt:
A History of
the Collection

BETSY TEASLEY TROPE

The final home of the Niagara Falls
Museum (and Daredevil Hall of Fame).

In July 1999, hundreds of people waited patiently outside the Michael C. Carlos Museum in the Atlanta heat for a glimpse of a collection they themselves had helped to acquire. This sneak preview of what would come to be known as the Charlotte Lichirie Collection of Egyptian Art represented the latest and most promising phase in the long history of the Museum. The future of the Carlos Museum was now inextricably linked to the colorful past of an eclectic institution founded 150 years earlier.

The Niagara Falls Museum (and Daredevil Hall of Fame) was created in 1827 by Thomas Barnett, a rather wily businessman and a collector of "natural and artificial curiosities." Barnett positioned his museum at Table Rock, with a commanding view of Niagara Falls, enhanced by a permit to guide tours behind the "Veil of Water" and an exclusive lease on the stairway leading to the falls. Even in the nineteenth century, tourism at Niagara was a lucrative, though cut-throat business, and Barnett constantly sought new gimmicks to attract patrons. On the heels of the Napoleonic expeditions and the increasing exploration of the East, Europe and America were consumed by "Egyptomania." Barnett saw the public's obsession with ancient Egypt as an opportunity to bring in additional tourist revenue. Consequently, he dispatched his son Sidney to Egypt in 1857, on the first of three trips to purchase antiquities.

Sidney returned from Egypt in June 1857, having visited the Valley of the Kings and other Theban monuments, describing himself as "a travelled man."[1] In 1859, in the company of James Douglas, Jr., Barnett journeyed to Egypt again and acquired at least two mummies. Writing an account of his honeymoon voyage on the Nile in 1860, Douglas would recall purchasing an excellent mummy "in double cases, for Mr. Barnett of Niagara Museum, for seven pounds."[2] Other sources report that Barnett returned to Egypt in 1861 alone, at which time he purchased four more mummies. Unfortunately, their new Egyptian exhibits did not keep the Barnetts ahead of the Niagara competition. Despite increasingly desperate attempts to draw customers, including a buffalo hunt staged with Wild Bill Hickok, that required eleven buffaloes and countless "Indians and lassomen with their horses and full hunting and war equipment,"[3] the Barnetts succumbed to bankruptcy. In 1878, they were forced to sell the museum to a longtime rival, Saul Davis, who immediately expanded the collections by purchasing the holdings of the Woods Museum of Chicago, which included five mummies.

Davis was compelled to move the museum to the American side of the falls in 1887, where it remained until the Shermans, a local family, purchased it in 1942. Another relocation, back to Canada, ensued in 1958, housing the collections in a former corset factory overlooking the falls. The frequency of the moves, along with their means of execution, wreaked havoc on the objects. Many of the mummies, coffins, and labels became lost or mismatched. The final move of the museum was reputedly conducted by dump truck, with coffins and mummies haphazardly piled in the back. As Barnett discovered a century earlier, tourists are fickle, and the mummies, fossils, and Civil War souvenirs were no longer drawing crowds. People now came to see the "Freaks of Nature" display, featuring a two-headed calf and other animal oddities, and the exhibit highlighting the barrels in which daredevils attempted to conquer the falls. The declining condition of the antiquities, the changing interests of the tourist market, and the extremely valuable location of the building combined to seal the fate of the museum, finally forcing the current owners to close its doors in 1999.

An earlier incarnation of the Carlos Museum, located within the Candler Library.

William A. Shelton touring the Theban monuments by donkey, shown here in front of the Colossi of Memnon.

Shortly before Thomas Barnett was forced to sell his museum in 1878, a small collection of curiosities and biological specimens was being assembled at Emory College. Founded in 1876, the Emory College Museum was housed in the library on the original campus in Oxford, Georgia. A Methodist missionary donated a group of Asian artifacts in 1894, foreshadowing the historical and archaeological focus that would ultimately guide the Museum. By 1915, the first curator of the Museum, Professor Stewart R. Roberts, had been appointed and had begun to install the collections in the new campus in Atlanta. Bishop Warren A. Candler, the university chancellor, presided at the opening of the Emory University Museum in 1919, announcing its mission to "preserve and display University collections of ethnic, biological, geological, archaeological, and historical material."

This mission was greatly furthered in 1920 when William A. Shelton, a professor in the Candler School of Theology, participated in an expedition to Egypt and the Near East, led by the eminent Egyptologist, James Henry Breasted of the University of Chicago. With funding from John A. Manget, an Atlanta cotton merchant, Shelton purchased approximately 250 Egyptian and Near Eastern antiquities. The archaeological holdings of the Museum expanded significantly in 1956, as a result of Emory's support of the excavations of Jericho and Jerusalem directed by Dame Kathleen Kenyon on behalf of the British School of Archaeology. The Near Eastern collection continued to grow during the 1950s and 1960s as several members of the University faculty, including Immanuel Ben Dor, Boone Bowen, and J. Maxwell Miller, participated in excavations in the Levant.

In 1957, Dr. Woolford B. Baker, a beloved figure around the Emory campus, became director of the Museum, moving the collections into Bishop's Hall and laying the groundwork for the extensive educational programming that has brought national attention to the Museum. By 1974, the Museum had relocated to the former law school building, designed in 1916 by Henry Hornbostel. By 1984, the collections of biological specimens and assorted curiosities had been loaned to other institutions, and the Museum had outlined a new mission, expressed by a new name: the Emory University Museum of Art and Archaeology. Michael C. Carlos, an Atlanta business-man and philanthropist, funded a complete renovation of the Museum, designed by noted architect Michael Graves. The new Museum opened in 1985, and the collections grew dramatically throughout the eighties, with generous contributions from Michael and Thalia Carlos, Harvey Smith, William Knight Zewadski, William and Carol Thibadeau, and Laurence and Cora Witten II. Rapidly filling its available space, the Museum was once again rescued by the generosity of Michael C. Carlos, who funded construction of a new building, also designed by Michael Graves. The Museum, renamed in honor of Michael C. Carlos, reopened in 1993 with nearly three times its previous space. Gay Robins, a prominent Egyptologist, joined the University faculty in 1988. Acting as curator for the Egyptian collection, Dr. Robins augmented the perma-nent collections and organized several exhibits focusing on the art of ancient Egypt.

In 1998, the Museum took a large step toward the future by hiring its first full-time curator and Egyptologist, Peter Lacovara. Soon after his arrival, Dr. Lacovara was contacted by Roberta Shaw of the Near Eastern and Asian Department at the Royal Ontario Museum, Toronto. A quaint, private museum in Niagara Falls was selling its

The main entrance of the Michael C. Carlos Museum, designed by Michael Graves.

Egyptian collections—would the Carlos be interested? After examining the objects, the Museum was definitely interested, though faced with a daunting fund-raising challenge. With less than two weeks to acquire the necessary funds, the Museum called upon the local media and the people of Atlanta. Both the media and the city responded enthusiastically, with the local papers providing front-page coverage of this unique opportunity and the citizens of Atlanta offering donations ranging from handfuls of change to million-dollar pledges.

Museum Board Chairman James B. Miller, Jr., and his wife, Karina, chose to honor Mrs. Miller's mother, Charlotte Lichirie, with a generous contribution that made this acquisition possible. The Lichirie Collection will be the highlight of the redesigned galleries opening in October 2001, an installation enhanced by generous loans and gifts from other sources.

The acquisition of the Lichirie Collection from the Niagara Falls Museum in 1999 and the relocation of the offices of the American Research Center in Egypt to the Emory campus in 2000 have sparked a new wave of "Egyptomania" in Atlanta. The Michael C. Carlos Museum has embarked upon an exciting new phase in its history, creating the finest collection of ancient art in the South, a source of pride for Emory University as well as the city of Atlanta.

1. Sidney Barnett, personal journal, June 29, 1857.
2. James Douglas, Jr. *Photographic Views Taken in Egypt—Winter 1860–1*, p. 33
3. Sidney Barnett Papers, *Business Correspondence, 1872.*

Death and Burial in Ancient Egypt

PETER LACOVARA

WHILE THE ANCIENT EGYPTIANS, in the popular imagination, are thought of as a morbid, death-obsessed people, this was far from the truth. In their own words, they referred to themselves as people who "love life and hate death." The purpose of the extravagant efforts the Egyptians went to, including mummification and the creation of sumptuous tombs as fully stocked as a bomb shelter, was to secure a literal continuation of this life for all eternity. These elaborate preparations were as much a way of denying the finality of death as they were to intended to ensure the continuation of existence through a complex series of rituals.

The Egyptians seem to have had conflicting attitudes toward the dead and their tombs, which became the object of both veneration and vandalism. In some periods, enormous resources were expended on burials, yet in other times only the bare minimum was undertaken. In some cases, economics was the key factor; for example, in the depressed economy of the Intermediate Periods, grave goods were kept to a minimum, although here and there, we find astonishing caches of jewelry in otherwise simple burials. Conversely, the imposing *mastaba* tombs of the Old Kingdom seem to have been relatively sparsely furnished.

Before the coming of Christianity, the Egyptians aspired to build funerary monuments that would be visible and receive gifts of offerings. Tombs were expressions of status during the lifetime of the owner, and social position was reflected on a larger scale in the cemetery layout. Tomb size and location were not only indicators of wealth, but also of familial or official relationships, as in the great court cemeteries surrounding the pyramids at Giza.

Pharaonic funerary display has its roots in the remote prehistory of the Nile Valley. Neolithic and Predynastic cemeteries show an increasing degree of social stratification over time, through the development of larger and larger tombs filled with great quantities of luxury goods, contrasting with a growing number of less wealthy burials. At this early stage, the basic parameters of the mortuary complex were already established. Sealed, dug into the sand, would be a grave pit or substructure containing the body, accompanied by provisions for the next world. Above ground was an earthen mound serving as a superstructure, beside which was an offering place for goods brought to offer to the departed. These essential elements—the burial chamber, the superstructure, and the offering place—could be elaborated upon and configured in an enormous number of ways over the millennia, but they remained the core of mortuary architecture.

Monumental funerary complexes consisting of a tomb and cultic structures for the reigning monarch appeared at the beginning of the dynastic era and for many periods remained the single most important type of project undertaken by the state. Royal tombs were usually in a separate location in the necropolis and were of a different type from nonroyal tombs, although throughout Egyptian history there was a constant interplay between private and royal funerary innovations in architectural design and ritual purpose. Although cult activities and offerings to the deceased were primarily directed on the tomb, the spirit of the deceased could also be honored through the temples or at other sacred sites via the dedication of votive objects and the erection of stelae, statues, or private chapels or cenotaphs.

An extraordinarily visual people, the Egyptians believed that a statue, a relief image, or even the name of the deceased might serve as an appropriate alternative home for the soul, should anything happen to the body. Mummification is thought to have developed from observation of naturally desiccated bodies buried in the hot desert sand during the Predynastic Period. With the advent of brick and stone tombs and coffins in the Archaic Period, corpses no longer in contact with the drying sand began to decompose. To forestall this, artificial methods of preservation had to be devised. Mummification slowly evolved to its zenith in the Third Intermediate Period, when it became an extensive and costly procedure aimed at maintaining the person's outward appearance in life, including the use of wigs and artificial eyes.

Egyptian funerary art developed as a means of preserving the likeness of the deceased in case some mishap should befall the mummy. Such portraits, however, were often standardized and idealized beyond recognition; presumably the name, although not always inscribed, helped to identify the deceased. Similar safeguards ensured that sustenance would be available to the deceased in the event that relatives or mortuary priests ceased to provide actual offerings of food and drink. These precautions took the form of deposits of various necessities, two- and three-dimensional representations of food, drink, and household goods, and inscribed offering formulae that, when read aloud, would magically sustain the spirit of the tomb owner with the essence of the material that had not been delivered.

The outward appearance of these rituals and provisions was more important than the provisions themselves. Burials could contain faux stone vessels made of wood or clay, empty food containers, miniature versions of everything, and so forth. Mummification was often treated in a similar fashion, with only a semblance of the embalming process being carried out, although the wrapped body in the coffin looked as good as one that had been "properly" prepared. These apparent shortcuts may have been rationalized by a belief that the act of performing these rituals was more significant than following them to the letter.

Such lapses may also hint at a lack of faith in the orthodox religion. Some inscriptions seem to question the value of all of this complicated mortuary provision and the ultimate good of funerary monuments. Nevertheless, the fact that we are still studying the ancient Egyptians in such detail shows the effectiveness of their burial customs. To them, to speak the name of the dead was to allow them to live again, and that is exactly what they have enabled us to do.

O OSIRIS N., YOUR SOUL STANDS AMONG THE GODS,...
WHILE YOUR NAME LIVES UPON EARTH,
WITHOUT BEING EFFACED OR PERISHING FOREVER AND EVER.
Book of the Dead spell, Plyte 167e

What's in a Name: Who's Who in the Carlos Coffins

JOYCE HAYNES

THE ANCIENT EGYPTIANS believed that the preservation of a person's name, or *ren*, was essential for eternal life. The name not only distinguished one individual from all others, but it had a life of its own. Ancient writings recount that saying one's name caused a person to live, so if one's name lived on eternally, then magically so did the individual. The funerary prayers and spells that request offerings, protection, and rebirth on coffins and other funerary objects, were addressed to a named individual. This magically ensured that they would receive all that would be necessary in the next world. Conversely, to erase someone's name was to jeopardize that person's perpetual offerings and, in doing so, his or her eternal spiritual life.

It was common for the name of the deceased to be spelled more than one way on Egyptian funerary objects, to magically cover all possible variations of the name. This was true even in the Old Kingdom. However, an extreme example of that phenomenon is demonstrated on the coffin belonging to Iawttayesheret (cat. no. 42), where the name is written in over twenty-five ways, each writing having either a slightly different arrangement of the hieroglyphs or using different hieroglyphs to create the same phonetic spelling of the name. The fullest spelling of the name consists of sixteen hieroglyphs and the shortest only seven. However, even in the shortest writings it is still phonetically spelled *Iaw(t)t(ay)esheret*; there are no nicknames for this lengthy name.

Names commonly had religious significance, and many were compounded with the names of gods. Some mean that the individual is watched over by a god, such as Pashedkhonsu (cat. no. 39) "The one that Khonsu has saved," or that one belongs to a god, like Ta-Aset (cat. no. 38), "the one belonging to the goddess Isis," or Neskashuti (cat. no. 41), "the one belonging to the god with two high feathers," namely the god Min, who wears the tall feather crown. Iawttayesheret (cat. no. 42) means "the aged one [namely Isis] is her mistress." A person could also be the gift of the gods, meaning it was the god's wish that they be born. This is seen in the names of the two parents named on the coffin of Iawttayesheret—Padikhnum "the gift of the god Khnum," and Tadiaset "the gift of Isis."

There are some essential components of inscriptions on coffins. One is the funerary prayer, which relates to providing the *ka*, one of the spirits of the deceased that lived on after death, with sustenance. The *ka* needed food and drink in order to survive. This prayer is usually made to Osiris, the king of the gods, but it could be addressed to any number of the great gods. It is called a *hetep-di-nesewt* formula and typically would read: "An offering which the king gives to Osiris, Foremost of the Westerners, Great God, Lord of Abydos, that he may give 1,000 jugs of beer, 1,000 loaves of bread, 1,000 oxen, 1,000 fowl, and all things good and pure for the *ka* of the venerated one, The Osiris [Name] true of voice." This prayer ensured that an endless supply of everything needed for the afterlife would be magically provided to the *ka* of the named individual. The titles of the deceased as well as of the parents were often included to further identify the individual who would receive these blessings and forms of nourishment.

The name *Tanakhtnettahat* painted over by Ta-Aset

As all Egyptians wanted to attain eternal life after death, they were called "the Osiris." This name likens the deceased to the great god Osiris, who was resurrected and lived eternally in the next world. Also, after the name of the deceased the epithet "True of Voice," or *maa-kherew,* was written. It revealed that the deceased had passed through the gods' judgment, and further that their final statements about living a just life were found to be true, hence True of Voice.

Several of the names and titles found on the coffins in the Carlos collection relate to the worship of Amun. Originally a local god of Thebes, Amun rose to national prominence in the New Kingdom when Thebes became the capital. Karnak, the largest temple complex there, was devoted to the worship of Amun and his family of gods. There were many thousands of priests serving Amun in the Karnak temple complex. In a papyrus of Ramesses III (about 1200 BC) over 81,000 people were counted in the service of Amun-Re. The priests and priestesses were mostly upper-class men and women who took on the religious roles as a sideline to their regular careers. Most were not full-time clergy, but part-time members of the temple who would participate only in special religious functions.

Tanakhtnettahat, "The daughter of 'Nakhtnettahat,'" whose coffin appears as cat. no. 38, is "Lady of the House and Chantress of Amun." The chantress in the temple would sing hymns and prayers during the frequent temple ceremonies invoking the gods, while others played the sistrum rattle in accompaniment. On the base in the area of the proper left arm the name *Tanakhtnettahat* is painted over, and a new name is written in blue over it. The new name is Ta-Aset, "the one belonging to Isis." One can easily see the old name beneath the over painting. Coffins were reused frequently in Dynasty 21, which must have been a distressing concept for ancient Egyptians, who counted on their own names on funerary objects enduring forever and ever. The titles have not been changed, and it is safe to assume that the new woman Ta-Aset, like most upper-class ladies of the day, was also a Chantress of Amun and Lady of the House.

The coffin shown in cat. no. 37 was prepared for a priest of Amun, as indicated by two titles: "The divine father of Amun-Re king of the gods," and "The Scribe of the temple of Amun-Re, King of the gods." However, this coffin has no name written on it. An inscription on the base bears the typical introduction to the name of the deceased, "The Osiris," followed by the titles, but the place for the name has been left blank. This blank space is followed by a clearly written *maa-kherew,* "True of Voice." This indicates that the coffin was prepared anonymously for one of the many priests of Amun who served in Karnak. A number of coffins made in this period were anonymous and included such priestly titles. While individuals with similar titles are named on other funerary objects, there is no way to be certain whether any of them refer to this particular coffin owner.

The title "The divine father of Amun-Re king of the gods" refers to Amun-Re of Karnak. It was *the* most popular of all the male titles of Dynasty 21 and occurs on more coffins than any other title. His second title, "The Scribe of the temple of Amun-Re, King of the gods," was more elevated in status. A literate person in ancient Egypt attained a highly desired "white collar" job. The functions of a scribe in a temple were many and varied, but most responsibilities centered around religious record keeping. The specific scribal duties are not enumerated in this title.

Another coffin of a priest of Amun is represented by the coffin of Pashedkhonsu (cat. no. 39), also of Dynasty 21. It is inscribed for Pashedkhonsu, "The one that Khonsu has saved." The name is preceded by a priestly title of Amun, and while indistinct, "The divine father of Amun" is one possible reading.

A nested set of coffins (cat. no. 42) dating to Dynasty 25 is inscribed to Iawttayesheret, "Great follower of the Divine Adoratrice of Amun." The expressions "Divine Adoratrice" or "God's Wife" or "of Amun" are used to refer to the highest level of priestess. This position was first held by a queen in Dynasty 18 but was later occupied by the king's daughter, and in Dynasty 26 the god's wife even held the office of High Priest of Amun, indicating that women were able to perform even the highest priestly functions. As the earthly wife of Amun, she could not take a human husband, and in the later dynasties she was required to be celibate. In Thebes her role was not only religious but also political, and she controlled large temple estates. Iawttayesheret, as a "great follower" of the Divine Adoratrice, would have been a woman of high social rank and of significant religious office, although the details of her office are not specified anywhere. We are fortunate that on the center front of the coffin there is inscribed a long line of family members of Iawttayesheret, going back to her great-grandfather.

An additional inscription is preserved on a wooden coffin post in the Medelhausmuseet in Stockholm, that is inscribed for the Carlos Iawttayesheret. This post represents one of the four corner posts that belonged to her exterior coffin that had a vaulted lid which originally held her nested coffins.

The family of Neskashuti (cat. no. 41) is closely linked in name and in titles with a different god, the fertility god Min. Neskashuti's name means "The one who belongs to the god with two high plumes," referring to Min, or Min-Amun, who wears the double feathers in his crown. Min was the ithyphallic god of fertility. His one title on the coffin is "Chief of the Singers of Min," no doubt functioning like the similar title "Overseer of the singers of Min." This title is well known as a male's title, although positions relating to singing and singers, were customarily held by females. The Overseer of the Singers of Min would lead the chanting that accompanied the procession of the statue of Min when the god went out to Thebes. Scenes of this ceremony are depicted in relief on the temple walls of the Ramesseum and Medinet Habu.
The father of Neskashuti also has a title associated with the god Min: he bears the more common priestly title "divine father of Min." His name is Paenmiw, or Pemu, "The one who belongs to the [holy] cat," referring to the cat goddess Bastet, who was popular at this time.

While names were important to the ancient Egyptians, they are just as important for the modern study of Egyptology. One can see how the names and titles on the Carlos coffins, once deciphered, shed light on the individuals who were once buried in the coffins. But more important, they bring to life those who once lived in ancient Egypt as we learn about their families, their towns, their livelihood, their social status, their religious beliefs, and their hope for eternal life.

Catalogue

Funerary Texts and Mythology

Funerary Texts
and Mythology

BETSY TEASLEY TROPE

FOR THE EGYPTIANS, death was a natural, acknowledged part of their world. This acceptance of death, whether it was viewed as positive or negative, probably resulted from the belief that only through death could life begin anew. Death still represented a passage into unknown territory, and the Egyptians created elaborate mythological cycles and funerary rituals in order to address questions and apprehensions surrounding this transition.

The Egyptians strongly believed in the magical power of both the spoken and written word. Through nearly the entire course of Egyptian history, from the end of the third millennium BC until the advent of Christianity, funerary texts and mythology were integral parts of the progression from this life to the next. The Egyptians referred to these texts as *sakhu*, meaning "that which makes *akh*." To be an *akh*, or transfigured entity, is the goal of every deceased individual. The *akh* is the spirit that, after death, has been deemed worthy by the gods and has successfully reached the afterlife. Funerary texts were designed to help the deceased achieve this desired state and were conveniently placed in close proximity to the body within the tomb. It was crucial that the deceased have easy access to the knowledge required as he or she faced the challenging transition to the next world.

The mythology of death was already well developed by the Old Kingdom, when mortuary texts first appear. The Pyramid Texts, inscribed on the interior walls of the pyramids of nine kings and queens of the late Old Kingdom, were a compilation of earlier, varied sources. Though originally restricted to royal use, the Pyramid Texts had filtered down to nonroyal individuals by the end of the Old Kingdom. These texts included incantations, spells, and formulae to be recited during the performance of certain rituals, underlining the importance of both writing and speaking in magical practice.

At the end of the Old Kingdom, another compilation of funerary texts evolved from the Pyramid Texts, with many spells taken directly from the earlier versions and others altered only slightly. The Coffin Texts were so named because they most frequently adorned coffins, although they are also found on tomb walls and less often on papyri. Since their use was not limited to the king, the Coffin Texts encompassed a broader audience than the Pyramid Texts, and for the first time, Egyptian mortuary literature expressed the idea that anyone could achieve the divine afterlife that had previously been exclusively a royal prerogative. A significant innovation found in the Coffin Texts was the inclusion of a "guide to the hereafter," giving the deceased descriptions, maps, and arcane facts that would facilitate navigation of the underworld. The most important of these "guides" was the *Book of Two Ways*, best known from a group of Middle Kingdom coffins discovered at Bersha.

Yet another new group of texts had been gathered by the start of the New Kingdom, consisting of nearly two hundred spells, many of which originated in the Pyramid and Coffin Texts. The *Book of the Dead*, known in Egyptian as "Spells for going forth by day," was heavily illustrated with vignettes accompanying most of the spells, unlike the preceding texts. Though the earliest examples were recorded on textiles and coffins, papyri became the most common medium, with the exception of certain chapters, which were inscribed separately on specific objects. Chapter 6, for example, is known as the shabti spell and is typically inscribed on mummiform funerary figurines.

Similarly, chapter 30 was engraved on the amulet placed over the heart of the mummy. The deceased usually included a selection of spells, rather than the entire collection. There was, in fact, no fixed order to the spells until the Twenty-fifth and Twenty-sixth dynasties, when the so-called Saïte recension produced a standard sequence.

A key figure in the funerary texts of all periods of Egyptian history was Osiris, the god of the underworld. The origins of this god remain obscure, and even the etymology of his name is undetermined. The earliest references to Osiris date to the Fifth Dynasty, when he is mentioned in the Pyramid Texts of King Unas, although the roots of his cult probably predate the Old Kingdom. It has been suggested that Osiris originated in the Delta city of Busiris, despite the fact that the god's primary cult center came to be located at Abydos, in Upper Egypt, the site of the first royal necropolis of the dynastic period. Consequently, Abydos and Osiris became linked to the deceased king. As the embodiment of the dead monarch, Osiris symbolized his resurrection in the afterlife. In spite of this early association with the king, Osiris was ultimately identified with the deceased of all ranks.

Osiris likely originated as a funerary deity, and as such, he was usually shown as a mummiform figure, with arms and legs wrapped in the mummy bandages. His attributes included a divine beard and wig, and the *atef* crown, composed of a tall, conical headdress flanked by plumes. Both the king and private individuals adopted these attributes, especially the beard and wig, in order to identify themselves with the god. Osiris was often depicted with a green or black face, colors that connoted both death and regeneration.

One of Osiris's primary designations was "lord of the underworld," a title that developed from the mythological story explaining his existence. Like the various groups of funerary texts, the Osiris myth incorporated aspects of other mythic traditions from different ages and sources, even though some of their concepts were contradictory. The most complete version of the Osiris myth was recorded by the Greek historian Plutarch in the first to second centuries AD. According to this account, Seth, consumed by jealousy, plotted against his brother, Osiris, the king of Egypt. Having trapped Osiris in a chest, Seth cast the box into the Nile, and Osiris drowned. Isis, Osiris's sister and wife, searched tirelessly until she found his body. Undeterred, Seth stole the body, dismembered it, and scattered the pieces in locations as distant as the Levant. Aided by her sister Nephthys, Isis again found her husband's body, with the exception of the phallus. Isis was highly skilled in magic, and so was able to conceive by Osiris, bearing their son, Horus. Horus ultimately avenged his father by vanquishing Seth and reclaiming the throne.

The Osiris myth reinforced the link between himself and the king. While alive, the king was the "living Horus," the son of the god. But upon his death, the king was equated with Osiris, the lord of the dead. Osiris was able to rule in the underworld as a result of his rebirth. Once ordinary Egyptians gained access to the funerary texts and rituals initially designed for the king, they too wanted to emulate Osiris by being resurrected.

As lord of the underworld, Osiris was responsible for judging the deceased and determining whether they were worthy of entering the underworld. Although the judgment concept occurred as early as the Old Kingdom, it reached its fullest expression

The family of Osiris shown in their standard positions: Nut, Osiris's mother and goddess of the sky, arches above her husband, Geb, god of the earth. Nut is supported by her father, Shu, the god of the air (detail, cat. no. 38).

Osiris typically appears as a mummy between his sister Nephthys and his sister-wife Isis. Here, the goddesses are shown with arms raised in their standard mourning posture (detail, cat. no. 38).

This scene depicting the weighing of the heart of the deceased traditionally accompanies Chapter 125 of the *Book of the Dead* (detail, cat. no. 38).

in the New Kingdom, as chapter 125 of the *Book of the Dead* and the accompanying vignette. A frequent subject for funerary art, especially on papyri and coffins, the vignette depicts Osiris overseeing the judgment of the deceased, carried out by weighing the heart of the individual against the feather representing the goddess of truth. Central to the scene was a large balance, with the heart in one pan and either a feather or a tiny figure of the goddess, named Ma'at, in the other pan. In most scenes, a demon called Ammit, "the Devourer," crouches below the balance, anxiously awaiting the outcome. Should the heart of the deceased prove to be heavy with wrongdoing, it would be eaten by the demon, and the hope of an afterlife vanished. Oddly enough, no depictions of a negative outcome survive, only the joyful individual being received by Osiris and presented with offerings.

Receiving a positive judgment from Osiris depended not just on being a good person, but also on being prepared. The prepared individual was equipped with the appropriate funerary texts that provided the knowledge necessary in the underworld. During the judgment, for example, the deceased was faced with forty-two underworld deities, each of whom who posed a question regarding the behavior of the individual on earth. The deceased had to address each deity by name and then deny having committed the particular misdeed. This situation required that the *Book of the Dead* be included in the tomb, since all the answers to these crucial questions were all contained therein, a "cheat sheet" for the afterlife.

Another of Osiris's roles, clearly related to his successful resurrection, concerned fertility, and particularly the production of grain, as evidenced by a peculiar type of artifact known as the "corn Osiris." The corn Osiris consisted of an anthropoid figure fashioned of mud and seeds, wrapped in linen, and covered by a wax mask (see cat. no. 5). The figure was placed in a falcon-headed coffin and arrayed with the attributes of Osiris, such as the crown and scepter. These "mummies" were most likely connected to the Osirian cult, in contrast to a similar artifact, the "Osiris bed," which accompanied royal burials in the New Kingdom. The beds were actually wooden forms in the shape of the god, filled with soil and seeds of grain. After burial, the seeds sprouted in the tomb, symbolizing the regenerative powers of Osiris and the expected rebirth of the king.

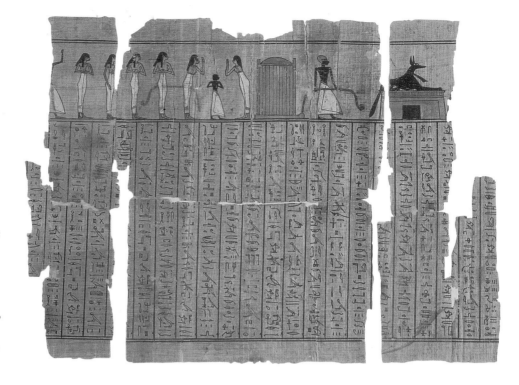

1 Fragment of a *Book of the Dead*

Ptolemaic Period, Second–first century BC
Papyrus, pigment
H. 20.3 cm; l. 28.5 cm
1921.90.1 A
Collected by William A. Shelton,
funded by John A. Manget

This fragment of papyrus is only a small section of a longer roll containing excerpts from the *Book of the Dead*. The spells and illustrations in the *Book of the Dead* were intended to guide the deceased on the perilous journey into the afterlife. An individual typically selected a few of the nearly two hundred spells to be inscribed on papyrus and placed in the tomb close to the body.

In this case, the owner of the papyrus, Paheby, son of Ankhpakhered and Takhebyt, has chosen chapters 1 and 72, along with others now lost. The text is written in a cursive form of hiero-glyphic, in vertical columns to be read from right to left. The initial spell associates Paheby with Osiris, requesting that he become like the god and that he receive the same life-giving offerings as the god. The desired result is that like the deity, Paheby will be resurrected. Chapter 72, entitled "Spell for going out into the day and opening up the tomb," guarantees that Paheby will be provided with a tomb and all of the offerings that traditionally sustained the deceased.

Above the text is a depiction of Paheby's funeral procession en route to the tomb. The central element in the scene is the round-topped chest holding the Canopic jars in which Paheby's embalmed viscera rest. A priest drags the chest, followed by a group of female mourners, two of whom raise their palms in the characteristic gesture of grief.

2 Statuette of Osiris

Third Intermediate Period, 1075–656 BC
Bronze
H. 22.5 cm; w. 5.4 cm; d. 4.4 cm
2000.15.1
Egyptian Purchase Fund

Osiris is shown here in his typical pose, wrapped as a mummy with his hands protruding from the bandages to grasp his emblems, the crook and the flail. He wears the *atef* crown, a tall head-dress with two ostrich plumes on either side. The fine, delicate, and attenuated features of this example suggest an early date, probably in the Third Intermediate Period.

In later periods of Egyptian history, figures of gods were left by pilgrims at temples and other sacred sites. These were usually small bronze statuettes, but on occasion, they could be quite elaborate monuments.

3 Oxyrhynchus fish votive

Late Period, 664–332 BC
Bronze, lapis lazuli, glass
H. 10.2 cm; l. 12.2 cm
1987.1
Gift of the Connoisseurs

This small statue group depicts a man kneeling before the larger figure of a fish. Resting atop a shrine inlaid with lapis lazuli and red glass, the fish wears a crown of cow horns and the sun disk. The distinctive appearance of the fish easily identifies it as the oxyrhynchus, a common African variety whose name means "pointed nose."

The oxyrhynchus is closely associated with the god Osiris, playing an integral role in the events leading up to the resurrection of the god. In the most complete account of the Osiris myth, recorded by the Greek historian Plutarch in the first to second centuries AD, Osiris was dismembered by his vengeful brother, Seth. After Seth scattered the body parts throughout Egypt, Osiris's phallus was eaten by the oxyrhynchus. Despite its participation in the downfall of Osiris,

the fish was considered sacred. The Roman author Aelian, writing in the second to third centuries AD, attested that fishermen took great pains to remove the oxyrhynchus from their nets, though tomb representations do show the fish being caught for food.

The oxyrhynchus was also associated with the goddess Hathor and was frequently portrayed wearing her characteristic crown, as in this instance. During the Late Period, there was a proliferation of small bronze images of deities presented as votive offerings in temples. The image often included a representation of the donor, as here, as additional proof of devotion. This fish was particularly sacred in the town of same name, Oxyrhynchus (modern el-Behnasa), as well as at el-Omari, the site of a necropolis for mummified fish. It is possible that this figure was dedicated at such a cult center.

4 *Djed*-pillar

Third Intermediate–Late Periods,
1075–332 BC
Bronze
H. 18.7 cm; w. (max.) 5.2 cm
1990.2.2
Gift of Edith Woodfin West

Examples of the *djed*-pillar have been found from as early as the Third Dynasty, although its origins remain a mystery. By the New Kingdom, the symbol was closely connected to Osiris and supposedly represented the backbone of the god. In both amuletic and linguistic usage, the *djed* conveyed the notion of endurance and stability.

Bronze figures and symbols such as this one were especially popular during the Third Intermediate Period and thereafter as embellishments for shrines or pieces of furniture. This example would probably have been inlaid into a larger composition, since there are no remains of tenons for mounting the *djed* onto another object.

5 Mask of Osiris

Late Period, 664–332 BC
Wax, bitumen, gold leaf
H. 23 cm; w. 11 cm; d. 16 cm
1998.13.9 a/d
Donated by the Brummer-Laszlo Family

The practice of planting beds in the shape of the god Osiris began in the New Kingdom. These planters would be filled with mud and grain that would sprout in the tomb, emphasizing the role of Osiris in bringing forth life from the earth. These evolved into a modeled figure known as a "corn Osiris." Such figures were sometimes fitted with wax masks with the face of Osiris. The wax itself was thought to have magical properties, and the gold symbolized the god's flesh. The hair on this example is colored with Egyptian blue to imitate lapis lazuli, the hair of the gods. These figures were placed in falcon-headed coffins and buried as votive offerings on feast days in cemeteries and sacred sites.

6 Anubis statuette

New Kingdom or later, after 1539 BC
Wood
H. 1.5 cm; w. L.3 cm
1999.1.138
Charlotte Lichirie Collection of Egyptian Art

The jackal god Anubis played a crucial role in protecting the dead and helping them achieve a good afterlife, and statuettes of this deity often adorned the tops of wooden funerary shrines and coffins. This miniature example may have come from a model coffin or a box for sacred oil.

7 *Ba*-bird statuette

Third Intermediate Period, 1075–656 BC
Wood, pigment
H. 12 cm; w. 3.5 cm
1999.1.139
Charlotte Lichirie Collection of Egyptian Art

The *ba*, represented as a human-headed bird, was a spirit form of the deceased that was believed to be able to depart the mummy and tomb by day, assume any form of existence it pleased in the outside world, and return again at sunset. Such figures were often used to decorate wooden stelae or other funerary furniture and were brightly painted. This one has lost most of its paint except for some traces around the face.

PROVISIONS FOR THE AFTERLIFE

The Tomb
and Its Provisions

PETER LACOVARA

AN EGYPTIAN TOMB served two main purposes: it provided a secure place below ground to house the body and a public space above ground where offerings could be left and the cult of the deceased could be carried out. These functions were relegated to separate, but usually connected, areas—the substructure, or burial chamber, and the superstructure, or tomb chapel.

Tombs took the form of elaborate freestanding structures of stone or mud-brick facades and interior spaces cut into a cliff face, or catacombs honeycombing the bedrock. The style and contents of these tombs varied according to the economic fortunes of both the tomb owner and the society in general. However, the simple pit tomb, consisting of a small grave dug in the earth, was the standard type of interment for the common man throughout most of Egyptian history.

Graves dating from the Neolithic or Predynastic Period (4800–3100 BC) were among the earliest found in Egypt, consisting of shallow oval pits dug into the sand and covered with a low mound. The bodies within them were tightly contracted, usually positioned on the side, and often naturally mummified by the dry desert sand. Artifacts such as ceramic pots, stone vessels, weapons, and cosmetic equipment were buried with the deceased, usually near the hands or head. Over time some burials became concomitantly richer with more grave goods, including stone vessels and ornaments, indicating a growing elite class. Many of the objects deposited in these graves appear to have been produced specifically for burial, including "costume jewelry," funerary figurines, and pottery that was sometimes decorated with ritualistic or funerary scenes.

In the Archaic Period (3100–2625 BC), there were great advances in tomb design that included elaborate niched brickwork facades derived from Mesopotamian architecture, and the first appearance of stone in architecture. The burials of the kings and queens of the First Dynasty at Abydos, as well as those of some high officials, were surrounded by graves of servants. Tombs were furnished with vast quantities of stone vessels, usually carved of calcite, also known as "Egyptian alabaster."

By the Old Kingdom (2625–2130 BC), the niched facade was simplified, with one niche at the northern end and one at the southern serving as offering places. This eventually led to the development of the "false door," a niche through which the spirit of the deceased could return to the world of the living and receive sustenance. These offering places were eventually incorporated into the body of the superstructure to allow the cult to be carried out in a protected area and also provided an additional surface to be embellished with painted or relief decoration.

Dynasty 4 (2625–2500 BC) saw the development of the classic Old Kingdom "mastaba" tomb, which takes its name from the Arabic word for a slant-sided, rectangular mud bench, which it resembles. These mastabas had stone or mud-brick superstructures with flat tops and sloping or "battered" sides. The earliest of these tombs had small chapels appended to the exterior and stelae showing the deceased seated at a table of offerings and recording his names and titles and wishes for provisions to be his in the afterlife.

These chapels eventually evolved into a complex series of offering chambers decorated with scenes of daily life, images of the deceased and his family, and funerary themes. Sealed statue niches, or *serdabs,* were also included within the superstructure of the tomb to house the sculptures of the deceased, which would serve as substitute bodies for the habitation of the spirit and models of servants to provide the tomb owners with food and necessities for the afterlife.

The substructure was reached at first by a stairway leading to the entrance to the burial chamber, but this was replaced in Dynasty 4 by a straight shaft cutting through the superstructure and into the bedrock below. These shafts were usually situated behind the false door. A multiplicity of shafts, false doors, and chapels have been found in the family tombs of the later Old Kingdom. The walls of the chapels were covered with carved and painted decoration depicting the tomb owners, scenes of daily life, or offerings for the next world. Despite all the elaborate ornamentation, even the largest tombs had very little buried within them: the deceased would be placed in a coffin with a headrest, and perhaps wearing some jewelry. Pottery vessels and items of food have occasionally been found. Tiny model vases in pottery and stone replaced full-sized examples and were often left in the tomb chapel as votive gifts.

The first major breakdown in Egyptian civilization, during the First Intermediate Period, saw a rapid decline in all aspects of society, funerary art and architecture among them. The tombs of even the most important personages of the time are remarkably crude and provincial. Typical funerary monuments of the period at sites such as Naga ed-Der consisted of simple brick superstructures fronted by small chapels housing roughly carved limestone stelae, which was all that remained of the elaborate decoration of Old Kingdom mastaba chapels. Grave goods consisted mainly of pottery and small stone vessels, jewelry, wooden model boats, and figures. These roughly carved and painted wood sculptures replaced the relief scenes of daily life on Old Kingdom tomb chapels.

The reunification of Egypt in the Middle Kingdom (2061–1782 BC) is reflected in a dramatic change in funerary arts. Large and impressive rock-cut tombs appear at Thebes, Bersha, and other sites in Middle and Upper Egypt. These are based on rock-cut tombs of the Old Kingdom with pillared exterior porticoes and chapels with false doors. Burials of the period were furnished with elaborate grave goods, including massive cedar coffins, wooden sculpture, and sumptuous jewelry. The effects of a weakening state are visible in the arts of the late Middle Kingdom, just as they had been in the First Intermediate Period. Elaborately decorated tombs again disappear, and funerary monuments and grave goods become simple and poorly executed.

With the expulsion of the Hyksos and the establishment of the New Kingdom, elaborate tombs reappear. The tombs of the New Kingdom were decorated both with relief carving and painting that were generally limited to the tomb chapel, although in rare instances the burial chamber was also carved or painted. The decoration, like that on the tombs of Middle Kingdom, consisted of both funerary themes and scenes evoking daily life.

At the beginning of Dynasty 18, the pyramid as a place for royal burials was abandoned as a safeguard to hide the pharaohs' tombs from robbers. The pyramidal form was then taken over in a vastly scaled-down version by nonroyal people. The superstructures of some private tombs of the New Kingdom incorporated a mud-brick pyramid. They often cap painted, arched-roofed tomb chapels with niches for stelae or statues. Many graves contained vast quantities of furniture, vessels, and objects of

On this scene from the side of a Twenty-first Dynasty coffin is a depiction of a pyramid-topped tomb in the desert. The blue tip represents a stone pyramidion that would have capped the mud-brick structure, while painted below is a round-topped niche that would have held a statue and below that is shown the door to the tomb chapel. Behind the tomb are dunes with dots representing grains of sand. Included in this composition are a Hathor cow, sacred to Deir el-Bahri, the location of this idealized mausoleum, and the god Anubis acting as protector of the tomb.

Detail of a tomb in the desert
Dynasty 21, 1075–945 BC
Painted wood
(detail, cat. no. 37)

everyday life. In addition, Books of the Dead, ritual and "dummy" vessels, stelae and sculpture, and funerary figures were produced for the burial.

The Third Intermediate Period (1075–656 BC) marked a sharp break with the sumptuous tombs of the New Kingdom. Burials of the period were often mass interments in family tombs or great caches in rough, rock-hewn chambers or mud-brick vaults. Many such caches of coffins belonging to the personnel of the Temple of Amun at Karnak have been found in the Theban area. Little in the way of grave goods can be found in tombs of this era, usually only shabtis, small offering cups, papyri, and votive figures of the composite funerary god Ptah-Sokar-Osiris. Stelae were made of painted wood to imitate more costly stone examples.

It was not until the revival of Egyptian culture during Dynasty 25 (760–656 BC) that tomb architecture and decoration returned to a semblance of its former glory. Deliberate revivalism is seen in the careful copying of motifs and styles of previous periods in Egyptian history. Massive tomb complexes were built at Thebes along the causeway of the Hatshepsut mortuary temple at Deir el-Bahri. Even though the tombs were larger and more lavish, they were still sparsely furnished with only a massive stone sarcophagus and shabtis. Painted tombs continue into the Saite Period, along with great shaft tombs containing massive stone sarcophagi and great rock-cut catacombs. Again, few objects were placed in these tombs, although the mummified occupants were spangled with great quantities of amulets and draped with bead nets.

The end of the dynastic period saw the development of the tomb chapel in imitation of houses or temples as exemplified by the tombs at Tuna el-Gebel. In the area of Alexandria there were great catacombs at Kom el Shukafa with painted and relief decoration of Egyptian motifs done in classical style. The beautifully wrapped portrait mummies of the Roman Period from the Fayum seem to have been buried in simple pit graves in the earth, while the tombs at Kom Abu Billou were rectangular mud-brick structures with barrel-vaulted roofs and a niche in the eastern end containing a limestone stela. The coming of Christianity brought an end to the tradition of mortuary monuments in Egypt, as a less literal version of the next life took hold.

Funerary Figurines

Betsy Teasley Trope

Funerary figurines are second only to scarabs as the most abundant of Egyptian antiquities. In Egyptian, these figures are called *shabtis*, *shawabtis*, and *ushabtis*, terms that are used interchangeably, though inaccurately, since each has chronological, and even geographical, boundaries.

Shabtis originated in response to the Egyptian view of the afterlife as an exact replica of the earthly realm. At the end of the Old Kingdom, wooden models of servants, and especially agricultural workers, were placed in tombs in order to fulfill the needs of the deceased. These models were apparently superseded by the first shabtis—simple, mummiform figures—during the Middle Kingdom.

By the Second Intermediate Period/early New Kingdom, shabtis were sporadically inscribed with Chapter 6 of the *Book of the Dead,* a spell that evolved from the Coffin Texts. This text, entitled "Spell for causing a shabti to do work for its master in the underworld," reflects a change in the conception of the figurines. No longer representing servants, shabtis came to be viewed as substitutes for the deceased. The Egyptian economy relied on conscripted workers to perform agricultural labor and maintain the complex systems of irrigation for the fields. Shabtis essentially became proxy workers, ensuring that the deceased would not be compelled to toil in the afterlife.

The New Kingdom witnessed an increase in the overall number of figures, as well as in the number accompanying each burial. Shabtis, with a longer version of Chapter 6 inscribed horizontally around the legs, were made of a wide variety of materials, including faience, clay, metal, and wood. Beginning with the reign of Thutmose IV (1400–1390 BC), the figures were depicted with tools in hand, typically a hoe and a pick, with a basket slung over the shoulder, giving substance to the agricultural aspect that had always been integral to their purpose.

Another significant change in both the ideology and iconography of the shabti occurred during the Third Intermediate Period. Rather than serving as a substitute version of the deceased, shabtis came to be viewed as slaves. The shabtis were then called upon to perform the dreaded agricultural tasks, such as irrigating fields and transporting sand from the east bank to the west. To ensure that the labor would be completed, one shabti was supplied for every day of the year, increasing the number in each burial to 365. Such a sizable workforce required management, and so 36 over-seers were included, each controlling a gang of 10 slaves. The overseers were distinguished by their "living" appearance, dressed in flaring kilts, wearing duplex wigs, and carrying a whip in one hand. The need for greater numbers stimulated mass production of these figurines, primarily of faience, mold-made with abbreviated texts.

The figures of the Late and Ptolemaic Periods continued to be mass-produced in molds, almost exclusively of pale blue or green faience. Improvements in faience manufacture resulted in shabtis with greater detail and refinement than those of the preceding period. Clearly influenced by contemporary sculpture, these later shabtis stood on a plinth supported by a back pillar and were characterized by slender proportions and benign, smiling expressions. The last shabtis were made near the end of the Ptolemaic Period. The decline of traditional Egyptian religion and changes in burial practices rendered the figurines, once considered invaluable to kings and commoners alike, unnecessary.

8 Tomb relief

Dynasty 6, 2350–2170 BC
Limestone
H. 43.6 cm; w. 33.6 cm; d. 5.7 cm
2001.8.1
Egyptian Purchase Fund

While the burial chamber was sealed after the funeral, the chapel above ground remained open to allow visitors to leave offerings and say prayers for the deceased. The chapel was often decorated with depictions of people bringing offerings for the spirit of the tomb owner.

The example shown here is of a rough style typical of the end of the Old Kingdom. Men and women are bringing offerings that include a goose and jars of beer. The inscription at the top contains a standard offering formula, while the texts in the lower register identify the offering bearers as the children of the deceased: a daughter, Irytnes, and two sons, Herheutef and Shepses.

9 Head from a statuette of a woman

Old Kingdom, Dynasty 5, 2500–2350 BC
Limestone, pigment
H. 8 cm; w. 5 cm; d. 7 cm
2000.11
Egyptian Purchase Fund

It was a popular practice in the Old Kingdom to place statues and statuettes in the tomb in case the *ka,* or spirit, of the deceased needed a home on earth. The mummified body usually served this purpose, but the Egyptians made additional images of themselves in case the body was destroyed. Rarely were these true portraits, but rather they were generic, idealized images.

This image represents a woman with an elaborate hairstyle still retaining traces of the original color. Egyptian women were traditionally painted yellow to denote pale skin from a life of indoor comfort, as opposed to the red skin of males, suggesting a tan from sports and labor outdoors.

The small scale of this head may also suggest that it came from a so-called servant statuette. These statuettes show people performing tasks for the deceased which first appear in tombs of the Old Kingdom. The Egyptians believed these servants could magically provide necessities for the spirit if offerings of food and other essentials ceased.

10 Model brewer

First Intermediate Period–Dynasty 11, 2130–1957 BC
Wood, pigment
H. (max.) 20 cm; w. (base) 9.3 cm
L1998.62.54
Promised gift

With the end of decorated stone tomb chapels following the collapse of the Old Kingdom, other means had to be found to represent the food and other necessities required by the deceased in the next life. To serve this purpose, model figures, boats, and scenes of food and craft production were produced and placed in the burial chamber.

Made of scrub wood and other cheap materials, these models were often crudely constructed and showed the stylistic peculiarities of the various provincial workshops in which they were produced. This example shows a woman preparing beer by stomping in a vat of mash. Egyptian beer was made of bread, lightly baked so as not to kill the yeast, and then mixed with water and left to ferment. The mixture was then strained and poured into jars. The dregs would be eaten as well, and both bread and beer were staples in the Egyptian diet and were frequent offerings to the dead.

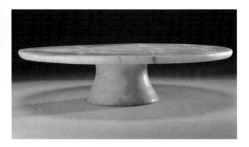

11 Offering table

Old Kingdom, 2675–2130 BC
Calcite ("Egyptian alabaster")
H. 7.4 cm; diam. 39.5 cm
1998.13.15
Donated by the Brummer-Laszlo Family

Tables such as this would have been placed on the ground or on top of tall pottery stands. They are frequently depicted in tomb scenes showing the deceased seated at a table piled high with food.

Offering tables appear in the Archaic Period and were commonly included in the burial equipment of the Old Kingdom. They were frequently made of calcite, although other types of stone were also used. While they are rarely found after the end of the Sixth Dynasty, they continue to be represented in offering scenes until the end of pharaonic civilization.

12 Offering tray

From Rifeh
Middle Kingdom, 1980–1630 BC
Ceramic
W. (max.) 28 cm; d. (max.) 6.4 cm
L1998.62.69
Promised gift

This pottery tray is modeled with representations of a loaf of bread, the head of an ox, and a leg and ribs of beef. More detailed offering trays depict houses with columned porches and a backyard piled with offerings. These so-called soul houses are derived from the simpler offering basins and both served the same purpose: to be placed in tomb chapels or on top of graves to receive offerings. The runnels or a spout carried off libations poured onto the tray.

13 Funerary cones

New Kingdom, 1539–1070 BC
Clay
L. 23 cm
1999.1.100–101
Charlotte Lichirie Collection of Egyptian Art

Cone inscribed for Merymose
Dynasty 18, reign of Amenhotep III,
1390–1353 BC
Thebes, tomb of Merymose (TT 383)
Clay
L. 8.5 cm
1989.6

Funerary cones were common decorative elements on the superstructures of tombs in the Theban necropolis, with uninscribed examples dating from as early as the Middle Kingdom. The form became more elaborate during the New Kingdom, when the name and titles of the tomb owner were stamped onto the flat end of the cone. Dozens of the imprinted cones were then inserted in rows above the tomb entrance. This arrangement was designed to imitate roof beams protruding from the front of the superstructure.

One of these cones adorned the tomb of Merymose (TT383), the viceroy of Kush during the reign of Amenhotep III.

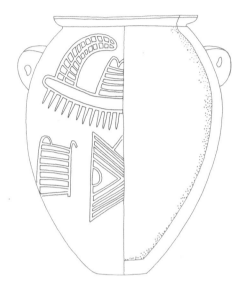

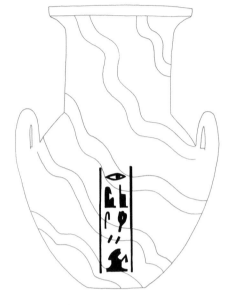

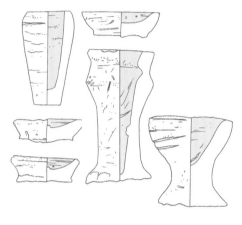

14 Vase with boat and mourning figure

From Abydos
Predynastic Period, Naqada II, 3700–3250 BC
Ceramic, pigment
H. 20.2 cm; diam. 16 cm
1921.21
Collected by William A. Shelton,
funded by John A. Manget

Predynastic graves contained objects used in everyday life as well as objects produced specifically for burial. Pottery vessels with specific decoration, such as this example, seem to have been produced exclusively as tomb offerings. The design on this jar represents the boat that carried the body across the Nile to a cemetery, along with a figure with arms raised in an attitude of mourning.

15 "Dummy" or model stone vessel

New Kingdom, 1539–1075 BC
Ceramic, pigment, gesso
H. 25 cm; w. (max.) 16 cm;
diam. (at mouth) 8.4 cm
1999.33.2
Promised gift

Model vessels of wood or ceramic painted to imitate stone were used as inexpensive substitutes for actual vessels carved out of a variety of rock types, and the Egyptians seem to have delighted in the intricate faux painting required to produce them.

This example imitates banded serpentine in the form of an elegant long-necked vase with side loop handles. The surface was given a coat of varnish to simulate the sheen of a highly polished stone vase.

It is inscribed "the Osiris […] sy," referring undoubtedly to the tomb owner to whom it belonged.

16 Model vessels

Old Kingdom, 2675–2130 BC
Pottery, calcite ("Egyptian alabaster")
H. from 1.1 cm to 2.2 cm; diam. from 3.4 cm to 6.6 cm
1921.38; x.2.28–38
Collected by William A. Shelton,
funded by John A. Manget

During the Old Kingdom, miniature replicas of full-size offerings were often placed in the tomb, either in the burial chamber or in the chapel. These inexpensive substitutes were thought to magically transform into their full-size counterparts in the next world.

Model dishes and bowls were the most commonly produced, but representations of food have also been found.

17 Blue-painted jar
Dynasty 18, 1539–1292 BC
Ceramic, pigment
H. 34 cm; diam. 15 cm
L1998.77.1
Promised gift

During the mid-Eighteenth Dynasty, a
new type of decorated ceramic appears
in Egypt, incorporating a rare powder
blue pigment derived from cobalt. The
pale blue imitated the petals of the blue
lotus, which were used in garlands to
decorate plain pottery amphorae. The
lotus decoration was not only attractive
but also evoked rebirth, as the lotus
opens anew each day with the sunrise.

The petal decoration could be combined with other motifs symbolizing
rebirth, such as the lotus flower and
ankh signs rendered in black on the
central band of this vessel.

18 *Nemset* vessel
Dynasty 18, 1539–1292 BC
Ceramic, pigment
H. 12.5 cm; diam. 11.1 cm
1921.16
Collected by William A. Shelton,
funded by John A. Manget

The ancient Egyptians had a number
of ritual vessels of specific form whose
use dated far back to the beginnings
of pharaonic civilization. One of these
types of vessels was the *nemset* jar, a
small, squat vessel with a spout, not
unlike a teapot, used for pouring liquid
offerings. This example has been painted
with blue bands to simulate garlands of
lotus petals, and a solid spout modeled
in clay has been added to the side.

Nemset vessels could be made of
pottery, stone, metal, or faience. Some,
such as this one, do not even have functional spouts and were obviously never
used for their original purpose.

19 Headrest
Old Kingdom, 2625–2130 BC
Calcite ("Egyptian alabaster")
H. 22.9 cm; w. 19.9 cm; d. 9.3 cm
1921.7
Collected by William A. Shelton,
funded by John A. Manget

This elegant calcite headrest, consisting
of three parts pegged together, was probably carved specifically for funerary use.
It would have been placed under the
head of the mummy as it lay on its left
side in the coffin. Other headrests, often
made of wood, were used as pillows
for sleeping during life.

As early as Dynasty 3, headrests were
portrayed on tomb walls and funerary
stelae, attesting to their role in creating
a comfortable afterlife. Further evidence
for the significance of headrests is
provided by their inclusion in even the
poorest burials during the Old Kingdom.
Ultimately, full-size headrests would be
replaced by miniature versions, amulets
often inscribed with Chapter 166 from
the *Book of the Dead*, promising protection for the head of the deceased.

20 Mirror

New Kingdom, 1539–1075 BC
Bronze, wood
H. 26.7 cm; w. 13.2 cm
1921.41
Collected by William A. Shelton,
funded by John A. Manget

In addition to being functional, mirrors, capturing the likeness of an individual, were thought to be haunts of the soul. The word for life, *ankh*, is the same as that for mirror. Most mirror disks in the New Kingdom were of highly polished bronze, so perhaps seeing one's face reflected in it would be a reminder of the transformation of the face into the golden skin of the god Osiris in the next life.

Mirrors were highly prized objects in life and were also frequently included in the tomb furniture. This mirror combines an oval disk, to copy the shape of the rising sun, and club-shaped handle of fine hardwood with channels for inlay, now lost, at the bottom.

21 Hippopotamus figurine

Dynasties 13–17, 1759–1539 BC
Faience
L. 1.8 cm
L1998.62.25
Anonymous gift

In the later Middle Kingdom small faience figures of animals became part of the burial equipment of nonroyal people. These figures frequently represent creatures who were thought to have some protective or magical significance. The hippopotamus was both revered as a symbol of the household goddess Taweret and feared as a dangerous wild animal. This figure, like most other examples, was probably broken to render it harmless when it was placed in the tomb. The lotus flower that decorates the head of the hippo symbolizes rebirth as well as the creature's swampy habitat.

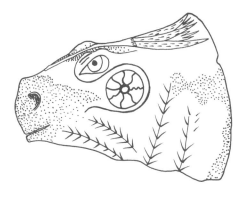

22 Votive stela

Probably from Qantir
Dynasty 19, 1292–1190 BC
Limestone
H. 8.8 cm; w. 19.5 cm; d. 3.7 cm
1921.12
Collected by William A. Shelton,
funded by John A. Manget

This fragment formed the uppermost portion of a small votive stela. The top of a double crown with uraeus is visible to the far left, though the face and body are completely missing. The name *Usermaat-setepenre Montuemtawy* is inscribed in front of the figure, identifying it as a deified form of Ramesses II (reigned 1279–1213 BC). The inscription continues to the right, stating that the stela was made by the scribe Paenmehit. No other figures are preserved, although Paenmehit himself most likely appeared below his name, perhaps kneeling before the king.

The Ramesside and subsequent periods saw a proliferation of votive offerings in temples throughout Egypt. Wealthy individuals would commission statues inscribed with their name, titles, and filiation, to be conspicuously placed within a temple. This allowed the donor to perpetually take part in the particular cult of that temple. Those with scarce resources might erect a stela such as this one in order to receive the beneficence of the gods and the offerings of temple visitors.

23 Uraeus

Ptolemaic Period, 305–30 BC
Wood
L. 14.5 cm; diam. 3.6 cm
1990.2.1
Gift of Edith Woodfin West

In its distinctive, upright position, the cobra embodied aggression and inspired fear. As such, it became the symbol most readily associated with the king, both protecting him and representing his protective capabilities. The cobra is frequently found as an architectural element as early as the Predynastic Period. The earliest extant example of a stone frieze of cobras occurs in the Third Dynasty pyramid complex of Djoser at Saqqara. In later periods, cobras wearing solar disks appeared atop divine or funerary shrines, often arranged in friezes. Tutankhamen's Canopic shrine was adorned with a frieze of composite snakes, their faience heads attached to gilded wood bodies.

Uraei fashioned from wood were also used for private burials, both in two-dimensional representations and affixed to shrines, coffins, and kiosks that were placed inside the tomb. This example is elegantly carved, with a slightly uplifted head surmounted by a solar disk. The sinuously curving body tapers below the flare of the hood, leaning backward in the menacing, prestrike posture characteristic of the cobra. The tail curves up along the serpent's back, extending to the top of the solar disk. A hole at the joint of the head and disk would provide additional support for the upper portion of the figure.

24 Shabtis

A. *Reis* shabti

Third Intermediate Period, 1075–656 BC
Faience
H. 14.1 cm; w. 5 cm; d. 3 cm
2000.13.2
Egyptian Purchase Fund

B. Shabti of a woman

Dynasty 21, 1075–945 BC
Faience
H. 7 cm; w. 2 cm
1999.1.126
Charlotte Lichirie Collection of Egyptian Art

During the Third Intermediate Period, as more and more figurines were included in the burial assemblage, the quality of shabtis declined. Molds were used to produce figures quickly and inexpensively, often resulting in figures with unmodeled backs and poorly defined features. Inscriptions were also abbreviated, providing only the name and occasionally a title or filiation for the deceased. An innovation of this period is the *reis*, or overseer shabti, charged with managing the large workforce provided for the deceased in the afterlife. The overseer was distinguished by his daily-life attire and the whip grasped in one hand, as illustrated by this example.

In both examples shown here, the texts are extremely faded, and that of the *reis* figure is completely illegible. The small shabti belonged to a woman whose name seems to be a compound incorporating the name of the goddess Mut.

A

B

25 Shabti of Padiamenopet

Dynasty 25, 690–656 BC
Glazed steatite
H. 16 cm; w. (at elbows) 5.8 cm
L1998.81.1
Promised gift

This shabti is an excellent example of
the figures belonging to Padiamenopet,
a chief lector priest serving under either
Taharqa or Tantamani, who constructed
the largest private tomb in Thebes
(TT33). His large, distinctive shabtis are
found in collections around the world,
though usually in a fragmentary state,
as is the case here.

Padiamenopet possessed shabtis of
three sizes and materials. The largest
figures were carved from various
unglazed stones, the medium-sized
figures were made of glazed stone, and
the smallest were formed of faience.
This shabti belongs to the second group,
being fashioned of green-glazed steatite.

The figure is inscribed with a variant
of the shabti spell created during the
reign of Taharqa and reads as follows:

The Illuminated One, the Osiris chief
lector priest Padiamenopet, justified
of voice, [he] says: O [this] shabti [if
one counts off ...] the Osiris lector
priest [Padi]amenopet, justified of
voice, [in order to do any work which
is done therein the necropolis; indeed
one implants an obstacle there as a
man at his duty: "here I am," you
shall say; count yourselves off at the
time daily to be served] therein, to
make arable a field, to irrigate [the
riparian lands], to transport by boat
the sand of the east to the west and
vice versa; "here I am," you shall say
if one seeks the Osiris the chief lector
priest Padiamenopet, justified of
voice, behold ["I will] do [it," you]
shall say therein the necropolis, for
I am you.

The piece had been repaired with a fill
connecting the two parts. At first glance,
the repair seemed satisfactory, yet closer
examination revealed that the bottom
portion of the figure had been reattached
facing the wrong direction.

26 Shabti of Neferibresaneith

Dynasty 26, 664–525 BC
Faience
H. 7.4 cm; w. (at elbows) 4.1 cm; d. (base) 2.3 cm
1998.11
Gift of the Connoisseurs by exchange

This tall, slender figurine belonged to
a man named Neferibresaneith, son of
Shepenbastet. Fashioned from pale blue
faience with a slightly matte surface, the
shabti is typical of the latest Egyptian
dynasties and the Ptolemaic Period. The
facial features are well modeled, with
almond-shaped eyes, and delicately
incised details. The mummiform figure
stands in the traditional pose, with arms
crossed, grasping a pick in the left hand
and a hoe and the cord of a basket in
the right.

The text, a standard Late Period version of the shabti spell, reads as follows:

The Illuminated One, the Osiris
Neferibresaneith, born of Shepenbastet, justified of voice, he says: O,
these ushabtis, if one counts off the
Osiris Neferibresaneith, born of
Shepenbastet, justified of voice, in
order to do any work which is done
therein the necropolis; indeed, (one)
implants an obstacle there as a man
at his duty; "here I am," you (pl.)
shall say; count yourselves off at the
time, daily, to be served therein the
necropolis, to make arable a field, to
irrigate the riparian land, to transport
by boat the sand of the west to the
east and vice versa; "here I am,"
you (pl.) shall say.

Coffins and Mummies

Coffins

PETER LACOVARA

Although a wide variety of timbers were used for coffins, the sycamore fig had special significance as the realm of the tree goddess, a funerary deity who combined elements of Nut, Hathor, and Isis. She is shown not only bearing food for the deceased but also providing a shady place to have a cool drink of water. This scene depicts a *ba*-bird sipping water at the base of the tree and the owner of the coffin receiving food and drink from the goddess.

Detail from the coffin of Tanakhtnettahat (see cat. no. 38)
Dynasty 21, 1075–945 BC
Painted wood

THE COFFIN was the most essential, and most expensive, aspect of providing for a dead person in ancient Egypt. Its purpose was to house and safeguard the body, believed to be crucial for the continuation of the spirit. The coffin was called the "master of life" and was often associated with goddesses, who were invoked as maternal protectors for the occupant. During the funerary ceremonies the "Opening of the Mouth" ritual to reanimate the mummy was performed on all images of the deceased, including the coffin. Model coffins could also serve as secondary burials for the departed and placed in sacred sites. The form and materials of coffins changed over time and varied according to the circumstances of the owner and the economics of the period.

Coffins are also referred to as mummy cases or sarcophagi, although the latter refers specifically to stone coffins. Ironically, the term *sarcophagus* comes from a Greek expression meaning "flesh eater," since coffins made of limestone often react with organic material within, causing rapid decay.

Containers for bodies in the form of rectangular boxes of wood date from the beginning of the Dynastic era. These boxes were either plain or paneled on the surface in imitation of contemporary tomb facades. The first mummies appeared during this period as well, although they do not seem to have been elaborately prepared, but simply wrapped in a way that preserves the outward shape of the body.

With the Old Kingdom, more complicated means of preserving the body were undertaken, and Canopic jars were placed in tombs, indicating the removal of the internal organs. Mummies were dressed in clothing, and their features were modeled in plaster or linen. Larger coffins in imported cedar or stone sarcophagi, some quite massive, were used in the early Old Kingdom. After the end of the Old Kingdom and the subsequent economic decline, coffins of the First Intermediate Period tended to be smaller, narrow constructions of soft, local scrap wood, painted and plastered or veneered to give the appearance of more costly timber. An innovation of the era was the depiction of a pair of eyes on the side of the coffin to permit the deceased to view the sun god rising in the east each morning. The mummy, wearing a mask over its head, would be swathed in many yards of linen and propped on its side to look out through these eyes. The masks could be gilded or painted yellow to symbolize the golden flesh of the gods, signaling the magical transformation of the deceased into a divine being.

This type of burial continued into the early Middle Kingdom, although the coffins and masks became much more lavish. Funerary texts, at first carved on the walls of the king's pyramid in the Old Kingdom, were painted along with other royal symbols in the coffins of the First Intermediate Period and have been found on coffins of the Middle Kingdom as well. Mummy masks evolved into a complete cover for the body that mimicked its form and became the mummiform, or anthropoid, coffin familiar from later eras of Egyptian history.

The Second Intermediate Period saw even more appropriation of royal symbols and styles in the so-called *rishi,* or feathered, coffins that have the *nemes,* or royal headcloth. In the New Kingdom, the mummiform coffin became the standard type of casket, and depending on the status of the owner, it could be nested in an outer coffin that in turn might be placed in an outer box or mummy-shaped coffin. Stone sarcophagi of box or anthropoid shape also appear at this time. The coffins were

As part of the funeral ceremony, a mummiform coffin is being held upright before a table of offerings, while a libation is poured over it.

Funerary relief
Dynasty 18, 1539–1292 BC
Sandstone
Gift of Elizabeth Elliff Snyder

Eyes of stone or glass with bronze sockets were inlaid into coffins of those who could afford them, to give them a more lifelike appearance.

Eye inlays
Dynasty 25–26, 760–525 BC
Bronze and painted limestone
2000.14 A–D
Egyptian Purchase Fund

decorated with bands of hieroglyphic text that imitated inscribed mummy bandages. The ground was painted white to resemble wrappings or black to simulate a resin-soaked mummy. The faces were gilded and decorated to represent the mummy mask. In the Ramesside Period, as a contrast, some coffins had covers for the mummy that made it look like a person in the clothing of everyday life.

The beautifully painted and lavishly furnished tombs of the New Kingdom ended with the Third Intermediate Period, and the focus of all mortuary provision came to rest squarely on the coffin and the mummy. The Twenty-first Dynasty in Thebes saw the most extravagantly decorated coffins ever produced, and their intricate detail of mythological scenes in shimmering color has been compared to the stained-glass windows in a medieval cathedral by one archaeologist. The religious aspect of the depictions is not surprising, since many of these coffins belonged to the priestly classes of the Temple of Amun at Karnak, which gave them access to the temple's finest artisans.

Despite their beauty, these coffins were poorly made out of inferior, often reused or local, soft wood such as tamarisk, acacia, or sycamore fig, and covered with thick layers of mud and plaster to build up the correct shape. They were, however, brilliantly painted in minute detail and covered with a golden varnish. On occasion, details of the surface decoration were built up in relief in the gesso substrate to simulate jewels and inlays. The coffins could be made in nested sets and inner coffin boards could be placed over the mummy, providing yet another palette for the artist.

During this period there were a number of mass interments of coffins in the Theban area. The most famous, of course, was the cache of royal mummies at Deir el-Bahri, but there were other deposits of coffins of priestly officials discovered in the nineteenth century. The Niagara coffins may well have come from such a tomb.

The later Third Intermediate Period saw the production of less elaborate coffins and the introduction of the cartonnage coffin as a cheaper substitute for wood. A wet mixture of gesso and papyrus or linen was placed over a mud body form, and when it was dry, the form was hollowed out and the surface painted and decorated.

With Egypt reunified in the Twenty-fifth Dynasty, coffins were again produced out of fine-quality imported timber. In nested sets of coffins, the innermost coffin was expertly carved to reproduce the sculptural form of the cartonnage coffins of the previous dynasties. The outer and box coffins were sometimes left undecorated to showcase their exotic woods. The mummies themselves were covered with elaborate bead networks imitating divine costume and bejeweled with amulets of gold, faience, and lapis and other stones. Many of these styles continued into the following Saite and Late Periods. Also at this time, massive stone sarcophagi placed in deep shafts were constructed in the hope that they would foil tomb robbers.

With Egypt's fortunes in decline again, coffins became cruder and shortcuts evolved, including placing cartonnage cutouts on the mummified body to simulate the appearance of a decorated coffin. In the Roman Period, panel portraits were sometimes substituted for mummy masks and placed over the faces of corpses as they were prepared for burial. With the coming of Christianity to Egypt, the religious basis for these elaborate provisions for the deceased was dismissed. But the coffins remain, still serving to preserve the identity of their occupants.

Mummification

SUE D'AURIA

MUMMIFICATION WAS MORE than just the preservation of the body, as when, for instance, contemporary societies embalm their dead. It was an essential part of the ancient Egyptian funerary ritual, which required that the preserved body be present in the tomb as the focus of the offering ceremony. Just as idealizing statues showing the departed as an eternally youthful person were provided for the tomb (and could substitute for the physical body, if necessary), so the body was to be preserved in a manner through which its owner would live forever in the next world. This often meant that more attention was paid to the outward appearance of the remains, rather than the process of embalming.

In its earliest manifestations, mummification was basically a process of dehydration. This was accomplished naturally in Predynastic times, when bodies placed in simple oval or circular desert pits, in a contracted (fetal) position, were dried out through their contact with the hot sands. Late in this period, about 3500 BC, the practice of wrapping the limbs in strips of linen was instituted. In the succeeding Archaic Period, as burials became more elaborate and religious beliefs continued to develop, there were rudimentary attempts at artificial mummification. Though remnants from this period are few in number, some bodies or limbs have been discovered wrapped with linen, the skin possibly treated with natron. Natron (ancient *netjry*, or "divine salt") was the basic ingredient of mummification. It is a substance composed of sodium carbonate, sodium bicarbonate, and varying quantities of other ingredients, including sodium sulfate and sodium chloride, or common table salt. It had many uses in ancient Egypt, including curing meat and fish; it was also employed in the production of faience and glass, and used as a detergent in the manufacture of textiles.

Beginning in the Old Kingdom, probably after the Egyptians realized that the presence of the internal organs contributed to more rapid putrefaction of the body, four of the organs (lungs, liver, stomach, and intestines) were removed through an incision in the abdominal wall, and the body packed inside and out with natron for a period of some forty days. The heart, however, was left in place, reflecting not only its importance as the center of intelligence, but its crucial role on the day of judgment, when the Egyptians believed that it would be weighed against the feather of truth. The removed viscera were treated separately with natron and placed in containers called Canopic jars, or sometimes into compartmented chests. Following the dehydration process, the body was wrapped, using not only household linens and clothing, but also fine linen purchased especially for this purpose, which tended to be used for the outer, visible layers. Protective amulets and jewelry were sometimes placed within the wrappings (though none were found upon the Carlos Museum's mummies). The body was then ready to be placed in an extended position, either on its left side or later on its back, into its coffin. The entire process, from death to burial, took seventy days.

Mummification during the Old Kingdom was generally restricted to members of the royal family and the elite, but as time progressed, changes in religious customs allowed more people the opportunity to have their bodies mummified. There were apparently several levels of mummification that could be chosen, depending on the financial means of the deceased. These ranged from simple wrapping to the removal of the internal organs by dissolving them via a purge through the anus, to the full treatment with an incision in the left flank. In the later Old Kingdom, an attempt was made to preserve the outward appearance by molding the linens of the face and body, and even recreating the clothing worn in life. Such features were occasionally applied to the body, over the wrappings, in plaster.

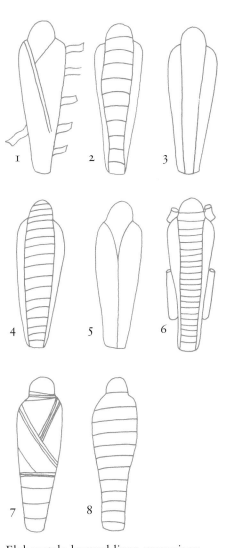

Elaborately layered linen wrappings were typical of Twenty-First Dynasty mummies. In this example, the outermost layer (1) consisted of an outer shroud held by strips of linen. Beneath this were alternating layers of tightly wrapped horizontal bandages (2, 4, 6) and linen sheets draped vertically over the mummy (3, 5). Under these layers, padding was placed along the sides (6), a lower layer was decorated with fine linen bands with blue selvedge crossed over the chest (7), and the innermost layer consisted of a series of tightly bound horizontal bandages (8).

Diagram of wrappings from the mummy of the scribe (1999.1.14; after a drawing by Margaret LeVeque)

By the Middle Kingdom, the process expanded to include the removal of the brain. After an early period of experimentation, the standard procedure developed was to draw the brain out through the nose with a long hooked instrument. The brain was apparently disposed of, as the ancient Egyptians believed that it served no special function. During the Middle Kingdom, a variety of mummification techniques were used. Some corpses were eviscerated and provided with Canopic jars, while others were simply wrapped with no attempt to remove the internal organs. Others show evidence that a purge had been used to dissolve the viscera, and finally in a number of cases, there was some attempt to draw the organs out through the anus. Arms were generally placed at the sides.

Further advancements were made in the New Kingdom, especially for royal burials, many of which have survived. There was a greater use of resin, derived from coniferous tree sap. Resin slowed down the rate of decay by inhibiting the growth of bacteria, and it had a sweet odor. It was poured into the empty cranial cavity and into body cavities, and applied to the outside of the corpse as well. Cosmetic treatments such as the replacement of the shrunken eyes with artificial ones of linen, and enhancing thinning hair with false locks, helped to create a more realistic effect. The body was stuffed with linen, lichen, and even sawdust to improve its shriveled appearance after the desiccating action of the natron. Many of the mummies of the pharaohs had their arms crossed over their breasts, while the arms of other individuals were generally placed at their sides. Most nonroyal bodies did not receive the lavish treatment that the pharaoh did, and the embalming was often very basic.

With the Twenty-first Dynasty, mummification reached its zenith, with complex measures taken to achieve the most lifelike appearance possible. Padding materials such as linen, mud, sand, and sawdust were introduced below the skin to plump up the corpse. The skin was sometimes painted, and artificial eyes of stone or glass introduced into the orbits. Strands of false hair, such as the braids found on one of the Carlos Museum's mummies (1999.1.3), sometimes supplemented the natural hairstyle. Attempts were even made to provide artificial limbs when necessary. The viscera were still removed, but it became the custom to wrap them in linen after treatment, and place them back in the body cavity, along with small protective figures of the four sons of Horus, protectors of the four organs.

Canopic jars were no longer needed, but their presence in the tomb was continued, as nonfunctional "dummy" jars. The wrapping of Twenty-first Dynasty mummies often conformed to a rather set pattern. First the limbs were separately wrapped. The succeeding layers alternated between thin strips of linen wound around the body and large sheets running from the chin to the feet. The basic outline of the body was maintained through the use of additional sheets and pads. The wrapping was completed with a shroud, often colored red during this period, bound with horizontal, vertical, and diagonal bands of linen.

After the peak in Dynasty 21, the mummification process began to decline. More reliance was placed on the use of copious amounts of molten resin, and eventually on external wrappings and decoration. In the Late Period, though the internal organs and brain were often removed, resin was poured into body and cranial cavities and applied liberally to the outside as well. Beginning in Dynasty 26, the organs were sometimes packaged up and placed between the legs, and the age-old tradition of placing them in Canopic jars was revived as well, though sometimes the jars were found to be empty. There was a decrease in the amount of internal stuffing of the body, but some was

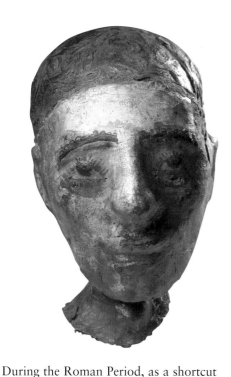

During the Roman Period, as a shortcut to creating a mummy mask, gold leaf was applied directly to the skin of the mummy, with the occasional addition of painted details, as in this example.

Head of a mummy
Roman Period, 30 BC–2nd century AD
Human remains with linen, gilding, and paint
1921.28
Collected by William A. Shelton, funded by John A. Manget

done with pads of linen, earth, and sawdust. The arms were placed in a variety of positions: along the sides; with both hands covering the genital area or crossed on the chest; or one arm at the breast and one at the side.

Though the brain and viscera continued to be removed during Ptolemaic times, some bodies were more carelessly preserved by a simple coating of resin, inside and/or out, and the alternative method of purging was still in use. The arms were generally placed along the sides, with the hands placed on top of the thighs. In the time of Roman rule in Egypt, the outer treatment of mummies included fabulous, diamond-shaped wrappings surmounted by portraits of the deceased, plaster masks, and carton-nage trappings. Unfortunately, such care was limited to the exterior, as the bodies themselves were given either minimal treatment or none at all. Some mummies have bones that are completely disarticulated, and others have been found to contain incomplete bodies, or parts of more than one. It is probable that these were in an advanced state of decay before treatment began. There are a few examples of elaborately treated bodies, however, that manifest the molding of the features in linen, or the gilding of the face or other parts of the body, an example of which can be seen in a head in the Carlos Museum's collection.

Mummification came to an end in the Christian era, when the practice of evisceration and brain removal ended, though some bodies from the fourth to sixth centuries AD. were treated with salt, rather than natron, and wrapped in shrouds. The practice, however, ran counter to the beliefs of Christianity, whose followers desired to distance themselves from the customs of the old polytheistic religion. With the Islamic conquest in AD 642, mummification came to an end.

Mummies and Modern Medical Imaging

HEIDI HOFFMAN, M.D., and SUE D'AURIA

Fig. 1: Mummy on the CT scanner at Emory University Hospital. An Emory radiology technologist, Heidi Hoffman, M.D., lead radiologist in the radiologic evaluation of the Carlos mummies, and Renée Stein, conservator, examine images as they become available for viewing on the CT monitor. CT-scanning is considered one of the imaging modalities of choice for the evaluation of mummies due to its ability to generate vast amounts of data without risking physical harm to the specimen.

THE FASCINATION WITH MUMMIES began in the nineteenth century, when many were acquired as curiosities by European travelers, often to be unwrapped more for entertainment than for scientific enlightenment. Mummies have been X-rayed since the 1890s, and major studies were conducted on the royal mummies in the Egyptian Museum, Cairo, in the 1960s. But scientific studies really came into their own in the 1970s, with the groundbreaking work of the Manchester Mummy Project, a multidisciplinary effort in England that has combined conventional X-rays with CT-scans, endoscopic examinations, and histological (microscopic structural) analysis. As new technologies have become available and refined, their application to mummy studies has advanced the field enormously.

While X-rays are invaluable in revealing skeletal remains, CT-scanning has added a new dimension because of its ability to evaluate structures of different densities, including the most delicate soft tissues. CT-scans are X-rays that are taken from multiple angles and then combined by computer to produce a transverse "slice" of a particular body structure. These "slices" can then be combined to create three-dimensional images that display findings of interest with amazing clarity. The remarkable preservation of some Egyptian mummies has made them ideal candidates for CT studies, which are totally noninvasive and thus cause no damage to the body. Past studies have documented the presence of even such delicate structures as the optic nerve with amazing detail. Current, state-of-the-art CT techniques even allow the creation of a "fly-through" tour, a virtual (computerized) tour through hollow mummified remains without risking physical damage to the specimen.

Endoscopic investigations have been performed in order to directly view interior structures of the body. An endoscope is a long, thin tube that is inserted through a body orifice and allows not only viewing of a designated area, but also the retrieval of samples for biopsy. Since the mummification process has desiccated the tissues, they must be rehydrated and cut into thin sections for further histological studies. In recent years, electron microscopy has been employed to enhance these endeavors even further. By utilizing these techniques, scientists have been able to document a number of diseases present in the ancient Egyptian population. Unfortunately, Egypt was not the utopia that is often presented in the beautiful tomb reliefs, and in this case, dead men do tell tales. Parasitic diseases were probably common, and they continue to trouble the modern population. Schistosomiasis has been documented as early as the Predynastic Period, and tapeworms, roundworms, and guinea worms have also been identified in mummies. Environmental diseases such as black lung (probably caused by continual exposure to smoky cooking fires in living areas) and sand pneumoconiosis were found, as well as trichinosis, malaria, and tumors. Since the mummification process often involved removal of the major internal organs, it is possible that other afflictions present in these organs, such as cancer, have not been identified.

The acquisition of the Lichirie Collection has given the Michael C. Carlos Museum an extraordinary opportunity to learn more about mummification and to advance the burgeoning field of the scientific examination of Egyptian remains. Such examination is not without precedent at Emory, since a Ptolemaic mummy acquired by William Shelton in 1920 was x-rayed in 1926, revealing a middle-aged man with no obvious signs of disease or injury.

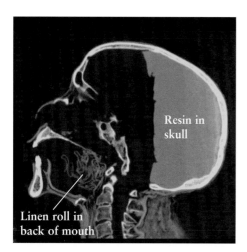

Resin in skull

Linen roll in back of mouth

Fig. 2: CT image of the skull of what may be a royal mummy. This image demonstrates replacement of the brain with a large amount of solidified resin, which was probably poured into the skull through the nose. Linens in the back of the mouth and throat were probably placed there in order to restore lifelike contours to the face and neck.

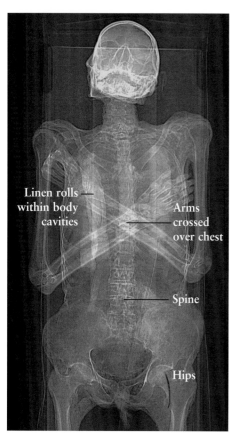

Linen rolls within body cavities

Arms crossed over chest

Spine

Hips

Fig. 3: Whole-body X-ray of the male who may be royalty. Although routine X-rays are best for studying the bony skeleton, shadows of the linen rolls within this mummy are also evident.

Between October 1999 and May 2001, all nine of the Michael C. Carlos Museum's newly acquired mummies were taken to Emory University Hospital for X-ray and CT examination (fig. 1). Though most of them belong to the later periods of Egyptian history, one mummy in the recently acquired collection (1999.1.4) may be of New Kingdom date. The type of preservation performed on this body is consistent with this date, particularly for a royal personage. The body is male, in an extremely well-preserved condition, with his arms crossed over his chest, right arm over left. The configuration of his left hand suggests that it previously held an object. Though a few mummies with crossed arms are known from the Middle Kingdom, these were placed with their hands flat against their chests. It was not a standard position until the New Kingdom, and then for royal males only, beginning with the mummy of Amenhotep I of Dynasty 18. The fists were clenched in order to grasp royal scepters, as in the mummy of Thutmose IV. The crossed-arm position recurred at a much later period of Egyptian history, at a time when the mummification process as a whole was in decline.

The Carlos Museum mummy, however, was given the "royal treatment" with a careful and elaborate mummification. The brain has been removed, and about half the skull filled with resinous fluid (fig. 2). Linen has been packed into the back of the mouth and throat, giving fullness to the neck and thereby restoring its natural contours. All pelvic and abdominal organs were removed through an incision of the left abdomen and replaced by five long, tightly rolled linen bundles found in the chest, abdomen, and pelvis (fig. 3). These were used as packing materials, and contain no organs, which would have been housed in separate Canopic containers elsewhere in the tomb. Through the use of advanced CT techniques, these linen bundles could be viewed as part of a "virtual tour" through the chest and abdominal cavities of this mummy (fig. 4). The heart was intact, the phallus had been wrapped separately, and a roll of linen was inserted into the rectum. The toes are slightly splayed, suggesting that they may have originally been placed in the gold stalls provided for royal burials. All of these findings are consistent with New Kingdom mummification for royalty.

There was evidence of arthritis in the neck and lower back of this mummy, suggesting that he was probably older than forty-five years of age. Although the teeth were in excellent condition, there was an abscess in one tooth, and a molar was loose. There was mild wear of the surfaces of the teeth.

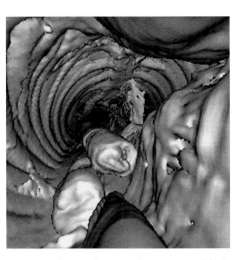

Fig. 4: Advanced CT techniques enabled the generation of "virtual" tours through the hollow mummified remains of the well-preserved male mummy. This static image reveals structures within the chest and abdomen as viewed from inside. All abdominal organs were removed and replaced with five tightly rolled linen bundles (arrow). As indicated, some residual pleural (lung) linings are also evident.

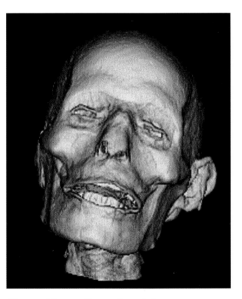

Fig. 5: Three-dimensional "reconstruction" of the face of the possibly royal male. This image was created by "stacking" approximately 218 CT slices into a three-dimensional model. The generation of these types of images allows for careful study of superficial details.

Of particular interest is the apparent destruction of the bony structure of the right mastoid air cells in the temporal bone near the ear. The inner portion of this bone has been eroded. In a modern patient, this would be suggestive of chronic mastoiditis, or inflammation of the ear, usually due to chronic ear infections. If it goes untreated or is recurrent, there can be destruction of the bone, as is seen here. This type of condition can now be treated with antibiotics and/or surgery, but three thousand years ago it could have caused widespread infection, ultimately resulting in death. Interestingly, the right ear is disfigured. Though the earlobe is intact, the top portion of soft tissue has been removed, probably as a result of trauma before or after death. This detailed evaluation of superficial structures was in part made possible by the generation of three-dimensional images from the raw CT data (fig. 5).

Five of the Carlos Museum's mummies are attributed to Dynasty 21. Surprisingly, only two of them exhibited characteristics of the high quality of mummification commonly practiced during this period.

The body of Pashedkhonsu (1999.1.15, cat. no. 39) has multiple facial fractures, including fractures of the right ethmoid sinus (air cells) and the nose, likely made during the traumatic removal of the right orbital (eye) structures. On occasion during this era, the eyes were replaced by artificial eyes, which, however, were not apparent here. A large portion of the brain remained in place and had fallen back in the skull, and the meninges, or coverings of the brain, were visible. There were several fractures and dislocations in the upper spine, probably due to rough handling during the embalming process, unfortunately a rather common occurrence. Pashedkhonsu suffered badly from dental disease, evidenced by multiple small abscess cavities. Many teeth were chipped or absent altogether. The crowns of some of the molars and premolars were worn down, a common malady resulting from sand and grit present in Egyptian bread due to the use of rough stone to grind flour. The four prescribed organs (the lungs, the liver, the stomach, and the intestines) had been removed through an incision in the abdominal wall, and the body cavity was completely packed with a mixture of gravel and sand. One or two linen packages, possibly containing viscera, were placed in the abdomen and pelvis, and a roll of linen was inserted into the rectum. The legs were wrapped separately before being bound together. No significant degenerative disease was identified, suggesting that this person was probably not old at death.

The body in the coffin of the anonymous scribe and priest of Amun (1999.1.14, cat. no. 37) was of indeterminate sex, as was Pashedkhonsu. This mummy, too, had numerous postmortem fractures, identified as such because no healing had taken place. Fractures were seen in the upper spine, chest, shoulders, and hips. The brain was removed through the nose, and the organs through an incision in the left abdominal wall. The chest was packed with linen, and the pelvis with many layers of gravel or sand. A long (18 cm) linen package in the body cavity may contain organs or may have been used to restore a lifelike profile to the body. The arms were extended along the inner thighs, but curiously, the wrists and hands were removed and placed on top of the inner right thigh. There was minimal arthritis in the spine of this mummy, suggesting that he was probably at least thirty years old.

The other three mummies presumed to be of Dynasty 21 date were not given elaborate treatment. A female mummy with braided hair (1999.1.3) was probably between

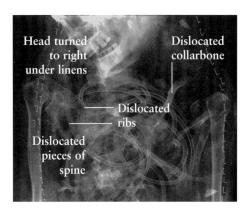

Fig. 6: X-ray of a low-level priest. This single X-ray provided a wealth of information about the bony structure, or lack thereof, of this male mummy. As indicated, most of the bones have been dislocated and placed randomly within the linen coverings.

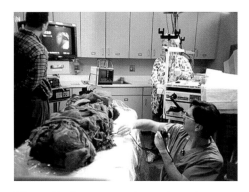

Fig. 7: Endoscopy performed on the mummy of Tanakhtnettahat. Dr. Steve Goldschmid, former Emory gastroenterologist, places a thin camera-tipped rubber endoscope into various defects in the linen wrappings in an attempt to explore the body cavities. A small clamp on the end of the endoscope allows for extraction of tissue samples. Observers watch the images on a nearby monitor.

twenty and forty years of age. Her mouth was open, and she was found to be missing several upper teeth, with additional fractures of her lower front teeth. She had mild s-shaped scoliosis, or curvature, of the spine, although it is unknown whether it was congenital or due to her position during mummification. Her brain had not been removed, but her mouth and throat were packed with linen. The woman's heart was very well preserved and, in fact, was the best preserved of all in the collection's mummies. There was no attempt to remove the internal organs; her diaphragm was intact, and her atrophied kidneys and liver could be identified. Linens were placed on her pelvis/inner thighs, and her hands were placed over the linens.

The mummy of a low-level priest (1999.1.11) was extremely poorly preserved, suggesting extensive postmortem damage. This mummy was essentially linens wrapped around bones that had been fractured and disarticulated and randomly placed (fig. 6). There was almost no preservation of the skin and no natural form or shape to the body. Though the skull was intact, the lower jawbone was displaced slightly, and several teeth were missing. There was no indication of abnormal wear or abscesses in the remaining teeth. The brain was left in place, and there was no evidence of organ packs that would suggest the removal of the viscera. However, there was a long (ca. 65 cm) narrow roll of tightly rolled linen placed between the legs, presumably as packing material. The hands were positioned along the inner thighs, a common position in the Dynastic Period, and the legs appear to have been wrapped separately. The feet, which appeared partly deformed because of fractures and dislocations, were extensively wrapped, the outermost layers with unusual braided linens.

Determining the age of this mummy is somewhat difficult, owing to its disarticulated condition. No osteoarthritis could be seen within the bones of the vertebrae, although there was one small degenerative cyst in the left knee. These findings, in addition to the lack of wear on the teeth, suggest that this mummy may have been between twenty and thirty-five years of age. It appears to be male, according to the analysis of Dr. George Armelagos at Emory University. The cause of death is completely unknown.

The mummy found in another Twenty-first Dynasty coffin was probably the Lady of the House and Noblewoman Ta-Aset (1991.1.18, cat. no. 38). The coffin was usurped from its original occupant, Tanakhtnettahat, a practice not unknown during this period. This mummy seems to have suffered from postmortem mishandling. The linen is tattered, and numerous fractures, especially of the face, spine, ribs, and pelvis, show no evidence of healing. The mummy's brain is totally intact, albeit shrunken. Even the meninges, or thin coverings of the brain, are present, suggesting that there was no entry into the skull. Many of the teeth were fractured, and one had fallen into the throat. Others were missing, probably falling out during Ta-Aset's lifetime. A small abscess cavity near the root of one tooth suggests prior dental disease.

It appears as though there was no entry into the body cavity for organ removal. The characteristic incision is absent, and the thin linings of the chest and abdomen are present. Because this mummy was relatively intact, endoscopy was performed by two Emory gastroenterologists to try and better visualize the body cavity (fig. 7), and several tissue biopsies were taken for analysis. The heart with its lining (pericardium)

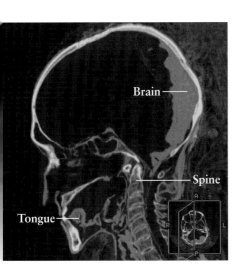

Fig. 8: Sagittal, or side, view of the skull of the body of a man as seen by CT-imaging. In contrast to the skull of the possible pharaoh, the brain has been left intact and has fallen into the back of the skull. The tongue and cervical spine (in the neck) are also evident.

Brain —

—Spine

Tongue—

was seen, as was a small, shrunken liver. A kidney was also tentatively identified, and the trachea was seen in the chest. The hands of this mummy were placed along the inner thighs, and the legs wrapped separately before being bound together. Though the muscles have shrunk through time, the stiff linen wrappings maintained their contour. A large amount of densely packed gravel and sand was placed in loglike configurations under the body but inside the wrappings, and between the thighs. Estimating the age of this mummy is difficult, although there is a suggestion of some degenerative changes in her lower spine as well as a degenerative cyst in her left kneecap.

A mummy of a child named Hori can be dated by his wrappings and coffin to the Twenty-fifth or Twenty-sixth Dynasties. The small size of this mummy (1999.1.1, cat. no. 43) led people to believe that this was probably a baby. However, the X-ray and CT-scanning demonstrated that both legs of this young child were amputated below the knees. There was no indication of bone healing, suggesting that these were traumatic fractures. Though they may have been related to the death of this child, it is possible that this mummy was "made to fit" an available coffin at the expense of his or her legs.

Based on the patterns of growth plates about the knee and eruptions of the teeth, this child was probably about two years old at death. The brain had been completely removed in a very rude manner through the nose, and the embalmers covered the resulting damage with a wad of resin-soaked linen. The organs were not removed, and the heart, liver, bowel, and left kidney could be seen. The arms were stretched along the outer thighs, the legs wrapped together, and there is possible evidence of a penis. Near the growth plate of the right elbow, there is a round area of "eroded" (eaten up) bone. In a child living today, this abnormality would strongly suggest a focus of infection, or "Brodie's abscess."

A second mummy of a child (1999.1.2) is datable to the Roman period by the presence of gilding on the skin. The child was probably about five years old, based on the growth plates around the knee and the pattern of eruption of the teeth. The brain had been removed with resulting fractures in the nostril and base of the skull, and a rolled pledget of linen or resin was inserted into one nostril. There was a slight overbite of the teeth, and what seems to be a bony defect of the central maxilla/palate, suggesting that this child may have had cleft palate. This disease could have caused facial disfigurement, speech impediments, and in severe cases, the inability to ingest food. Though there are several other documented cases from ancient Egypt, they are not common.

There was a fracture of the skull, extending from front to back, and a second fracture of the right femur (thigh bone) just above the knee. As these are the only fractures identified on this mummy, one might speculate that they may be related to the death of this child, as mummies who have been mishandled have innumerable fractures, whereas this one has only these isolated two.

The heart has been left in place, with dense packing material, including folded linens, resin, and perhaps stones, in the chest. The organs seem to have been removed through one of two defects in the skin, and the viscera were absent, probably housed separately in Canopic jars. There is the suggestion of a small, desiccated phallus. Rolls of linens were placed between the legs, which were wrapped separately and then bound together. The mummy's arms and hands are outstretched along the outer thighs.

The decline of the art of mummification is apparent in the body of a man (1999.1.5) who lived during the Roman Period. He had been designated "the General" at the Niagara Falls Museum, although we have no specific evidence to indicate his position or status. His very mild degenerative disease of the spine suggests an age at death of at least thirty-five. His arms were placed along his outer thighs, and the legs were not separately wrapped, but bound as a unit. Though the body is extremely well preserved, there was no attempt to remove the internal organs or brain (fig. 8). The intact skin surface was densely smeared with resin, and the soft organs were remarkably well preserved, particularly the phallus and musculature of the thighs. The liver and left kidney were definitively identified, and the linings of the bowel could be seen in the abdomen and pelvis. Within the chest are pleural linings that covered the lungs, and though little actual heart tissue could be identified, the pericardium, or covering of the heart, was present. A fascinating find was the presence of innumerable soft tissue calcifications in the musculature of the thighs and armpits, which most likely reflects a parasitic infection (fig. 9). The most likely culprit is cysticercosis, a tapeworm (*Taenia solium*) that can be picked up by eating infected pork. The calcifications have the shape, size, and orientation of typical tapeworm cysts; when the parasite dies, it calcifies. If widespread, this disease could have caused this man to suffer from blurry or disturbed vision, imbalance, and even seizures. However, typically the muscle calcifications are asymptomatic, and most people have symptoms only when the parasite invades the eyes and brain, which was apparently not the case here.

The above descriptions highlight only some of the mummies' secrets uncovered by careful and rigorous scientific investigation. As the study of mummies continues to evolve as a multidisciplinary endeavor, we can expect to learn more about the life, death, and postmortem treatment of these fascinating members of antiquity.

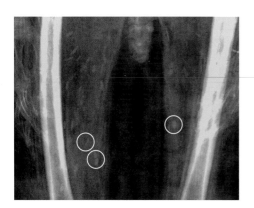

Fig. 9: X-ray of the legs of "the General," demonstrating remarkable preservation of soft tissues. Circles indicate numerous rounded calcifications that likely reflect cysticercosis, a parasitic infection caused by a pork tapeworm. The parasite enters the musculature and calcifies upon death. Although these calcifications may have been felt underneath the skin, they were likely asymptomatic. On the contrary, similar infection elsewhere in this man, for example, in the brain or eyes, would most likely have caused neurologic symptoms.

27 Embalming materials

A. Knife
Old Kingdom or later, after 2675 BC
Obsidian
L. 24.5 cm; w. 5.5 cm
1971.102 A
Gift of Dr. Thomas H. English

B. Bandage
Third Intermediate Period, 1075–656 BC
Linen
H. 54 cm; w. 53 cm
1999.1.14
Charlotte Lichirie Collection of Egyptian Art

C. Natron
From Wadi Natrun
Gift of Dr. Bob Brier

D. Inscribed mummy bandage
Ptolemaic Period, 305–30 BC
Linen
H. 8 cm; w. 22 cm
1921.61
Collected by William A. Shelton,
funded by John A. Manget

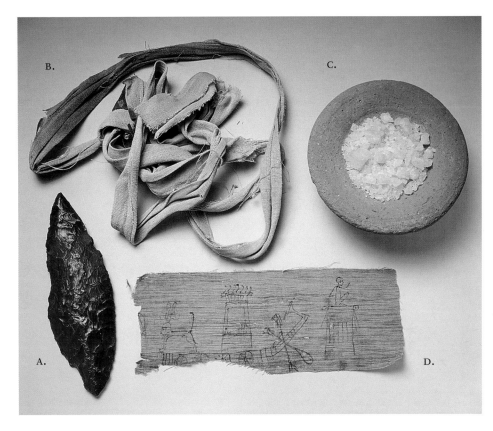

Ritual texts specify a "black stone" knife as the tool that should be used by the embalmer to make the incision to remove the internal organs. Obsidian, a volcanic glass, fractures to create an edge sharper than surgical steel, and thus served as an ideal cutting instrument.

Natron, a naturally occurring salt usually consisting of sodium bicarbonate or sodium chloride, was the chief ingredient employed in drying and preserving the mummy. It was placed over the skin of the mummy as well as inside the body cavity during the process of embalming. It was also used as a cleansing agent and signified purity.

Once the body was prepared, a process that ideally took seventy days, it would be wrapped in yards and yards of linen bandages. These sometimes served as writing surfaces for the *Book of the Dead*, substituting for expensive papyrus rolls. This bandage has a scene in black ink of a funerary boat on wheels, part of a procession to the tomb.

28. Jar of resin (not pictured)
Second Intermediate Period, 1630–1539/23 BC
Ceramic, linen, cartonnage
H. 7.9 cm; diam. (rim) 5.1 cm
1999.1.104
Charlotte Lichirie Collection of Egyptian Art

Tree resins poured over the mummy and its coffin would darken and harden to a substance that was mistaken for bitumen, or in Arabic "mummiya," hence the term *mummy*. This vessel still has the remains of a linen and cartonnage seal to secure the contents. The vase has been handmade in the Nubian ceramic tradition and may have belonged to one of the Nubian troops who were employed by the Egyptian army in the wars against the invading Hyksos.

29 Set of "dummy" Canopic jars

Third Intermediate Period, ca. 1075–656 BC
Limestone
Jackal: H. 39 cm; diam. (max.) 12.5 cm
Human: H. 38 cm; diam. (max.) 12.5 cm
Falcon: H. 36 cm; diam. (max.) 12.5 cm
Baboon: H. 34 cm; diam. (max.) 12.5 cm
1999.1.29–32
Charlotte Lichirie Collection of Egyptian Art

One of the innovations in mummification in Dynasty 21 involved placing
the mummified internal organs back in
the body. However, Canopic jars had
become such a standard part of burial
equipment that model jars were still
placed in the tomb. This set of jars has
separate lids, but the insides of the jars
are not hollowed out. The images on
the lids represent the four sons of the
god Horus, who protected the internal
organs of the mummy: they were the
baboon-headed Hapy, protector of the
lungs; the jackal-headed Duamutef,
guardian of the stomach: the human-
headed Imsety, keeper of the liver; and
the falcon-headed Qebehsenuef, protector
of the intestines. The awkward carving
of the lids is typical of the period, and
traces of the original pigment that decorated them appears to lie under nineteenth-century polychrome overpainting.

30 "Dummy" Canopic jar

Third Intermediate Period, 1075–656 BC
Limestone, pigment
H. 24 cm; w. 9 cm
1999.1.27
Charlotte Lichirie Collection of Egyptian Art

Yet another version of the simulated
Canopic jars of the Third Intermediate
Period is this example, which could not
even open, as the lid and the base are
joined and carved from a single piece of
stone. This jar is topped by a human-
headed lid, representing the god Imsety,
who protected the liver. Traces of the
original black pigment that detailed the
eyes and facial features can still be seen.

31 Coffin and mummy (not pictured)

From Abydos
Dynasty 4, ca. 2625–2500 BC
Cedar, linen, human remains
Coffin: L. 177.2 cm; w. 49.5 cm; d. 5.7 cm
Mummy: L. 142.2 cm; w. 48.3 cm; d. 27.3 cm
1921.1
Collected by William A. Shelton,
funded by John A. Manget

The first attempts at mummification
were necessitated by the development
of larger and more elaborate tombs and
coffins, which counteracted the drying
effects of the desert sand. In this early
period there was more of an attempt
to preserve the form of the body in the
wrappings rather than treating the body
itself. The fingers and toes were individ-
ually wrapped, as were the arms and
legs. By the end of the Old Kingdom,
members of the provincial nobility were
buried in their local cemeteries rather
than in the great court necropoleis at Giza
and Saqqara as they had been earlier.

Although now badly deteriorated, this
mummy was once carefully wrapped in
multiple layers of fine linen bands. The
coffin was made of massive cedar planks
doweled together, and the outer surfaces
of the boards were left undecorated and
uninscribed. The name of the owner of
this coffin is not known, and the mastaba at Abydos from which it came was
not recorded.

32 Coffin of Nebetit

From Assiut
Late Dynasty 11, 1957–1938 BC
Wood, pigment
L. 106.5 cm; w. 41.3 cm; d. 50.8 cm
1921.2
Collected by William A. Shelton,
funded by John A. Manget

With the breakdown of the central gov-
ernment in the First Intermediate Period,
fine timber was no longer imported into
Egypt from the Levant. This coffin is
made out of scraps of local wood pegged
together and coated with gesso and
painted yellow-brown to look like a fine
piece of cabinetry. It is decorated with a
pair of eyes through which the mummy
could magically see.

Bands of text are inscribed with hieroglyphs executed in the crude, almost
cartoonlike, style of the period. They
recount the versions of the classic offering formula, the top band above the eyes
reading:

> An offering that the king may give
> through Osiris, lord of Busiris first of
> the westerners, lord of Abydos, on his
> thrones; an offering of beef and fowl,
> bread and beer to the ka of the
> deceased, may she be honored by
> the great god, the lord of heaven on
> his thrones, the deceased, Nebetit.

Other inscriptions on the sides and lid
of the coffin invoke the god Anubis and
other deities on behalf of the deceased.

33 Model coffin

Dynasty 12, 1938–1759 BC
Wood, pigment
L. 16.3 cm; w. 5.2 cm; d. 4.7 cm (at feet)
1998.16.2
Anonymous gift

The mummy-shaped coffin first appears in the Middle Kingdom. This miniature model coffin may have been made to lie on a bier on board a model funeral boat or to serve as a votive substitute for the actual coffin. The wig, face, and collar represent a mummy mask over a bandaged body; this configuration later developed into the familiar anthropoid coffin. Often such coffins were placed inside an outer box coffin and propped on their sides so that they could peer through the eyes painted on the side in the same manner as a mummy.

This example is shown with a full wig typically worn by women of the period. At her throat, she wears a magical *sweret* bead for protection and a broad collar. A column of text runs down the front, which reads:

> An offering which the king gives to Anubis who is upon his mountain, who is in his wrappings [...].

34 Lid of a mummiform coffin

Dynasty 18, 1539–1075 BC
Wood, gilt, pigment, linen
L. 82 cm; w. 44.5 cm; d. 19 cm
1999.40
Promised gift

By the New Kingdom the anthropoid, or mummy-shaped, coffin became the standard casket used for king and commoner alike. This elaborate black and gold coffin is of a type popular from the middle to the end of the Eighteenth Dynasty. The gilded face and blue striped hair depict the deceased as a divine being, and by this period a departed person was often referred to as an "Osiris."

The body of the coffin is colored black with a tree resin to symbolize the realm of the underworld. Bands of yellow text running along the sides simulated inscribed mummy bandages. A floral broad collar is depicted hanging below the neck with lotus terminals and rows of blue, red, and gold beads below that; the vulture goddess, wings outstretched to protect the deceased, has been applied in gilded cartonnage to the chest of the coffin lid.

The gold used in the face, in the collar, and on the vulture has a reddish tinge, possibly an association with the rising sun to invoke rebirth. The lower half of the lid was cut down in modern times and has been restored.

35 Arm from a coffin

Dynasty 20, 1190–1075 BC
Wood, pigment
L. 37 cm; w. 7.8 cm
L1998.82
Lent by Yvonne Markowitz

During the later Ramesside Period some uniquely styled coffins depicted the deceased not as a mummy, but in everyday costume. These were more often depicted under the lid on a wooden body cover placed over the mummy.

This arm would have belonged to a cover made for a woman and shows an elegant hand with rings of varying materials on each finger and a polychrome beaded bracelet. It was made separately and would have been attached to a large board carved and painted to simulate a pleated linen dress.

36 Coffin board

Dynasty 21, 1075–945 BC
Wood, pigment
L. 162.5 cm; w. 37 cm; d. 9 cm
1999.1.12
Charlotte Lichirie Collection of Egyptian Art

Coffin boards were a feature largely confined to the Twenty-first Dynasty and evolved out of the mummy masks and elaborate body covers of the New Kingdom. The coffin board looked like, and served as, a secondary lid and was covered with depictions of gods and amuletic devices to protect the mummy, which rested underneath it.

This beautifully preserved example depicts a female in a full wig wearing a jeweled broad collar with falcon terminals and pectorals of winged scarabs. Her arms are rendered as crossed and wearing beaded bracelets, and the fingers of her folded hands are bedecked with rings.

The sky goddess stretches across the middle of the board, and two columns of text, a standard offering formula, run below. The inscription enumerates several epithets of Osiris and requests offerings on behalf of the deceased. The name of the deceased is not included, which was frequently the case on coffins manufactured or purchased at the last minute.

The text is flanked by images of Osiris, Sokar, *ba*-birds and *wedjat*-eyes. With the appearance of cartonnage coffins in Dynasty 22 and later, the ungainly coffin board disappears and is ultimately replaced by intricate bead networks that appear on the mummy in Dynasty 25 and later.

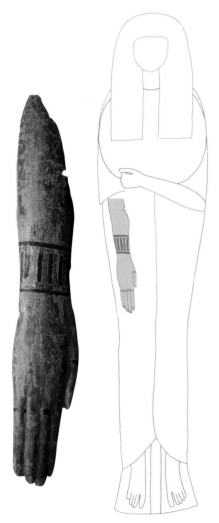

37 Coffin and mummy of a priestly official

Dynasty 21, 1070–946 BC
Wood, pigment, linen, human remains
Coffin: L. 187 cm; w. 54 cm; d. 28 cm
Mummy: L. 140 cm; w. 38 cm; d. 23 cm
1999.1.13 (coffin); 1999.1.14 (mummy)
Charlotte Lichirie Collection of Egyptian Art

This coffin appears to have been made for a priestly official in the temple of Amun at Karnak, but it was never finished. The hieroglyphic text that would have recorded the name of the owner was left blank, although it does bear the titles of priest ("god's father") and scribe. In addition, the coffin never received its outer coat of yellow varnish, leaving the colors, particularly the "Egyptian blue," as vivid as the day they were painted. While most colors used by the ancient Egyptians were simple mineral pigments, this bright blue is a ground glass-frit colored with copper. This process produced a remarkably stable blue and was prized throughout the ancient world.

The sides of the coffin have been painted in a broad and lively hand, made more vivid by the lack of surface coating. Unfortunately, probably due to this lack of protection, the painted gesso surface of the lid has been almost entirely lost, leaving nothing but bare wood. The head end decoration has also been lost, but fortunately the sides are well preserved and include scenes of Hathor of Deir el-Bahri and other gods and goddesses, including Re, Osiris, Anubis, and Nut. On the proper left, beginning at the foot end, is a depiction of a pyramid-topped tomb in the desert with a large image of a Hathor cow in front. After this are images of Osiris, Isis, and Nephthys worshipping the Abydos fetish and images of Re, Osiris, and the goddess of the west adoring another Abydos fetish.

On the proper left side of the coffin are images of Nut and Osiris, Anubis, Osiris, Re, and a winged scarab over a depiction of the evil serpent Apophis, his body cut with many knives. At the foot end is another rendering of a pyramid-topped tomb with a Hathor cow, here fronted by an image of Anubis. The interior painting is largely obscured by remains of the mummy wrappings stuck with resin, although traces of an image of the goddess of the west are still visible on the floor. The resin also seeped into, and discolored, the sides of the coffin. However, the images still visible on the interior sides were boldly drawn with figures of Osiris and gods of the underworld and with an image of a *ba*-bird with outstretched wings at the head end of the coffin.

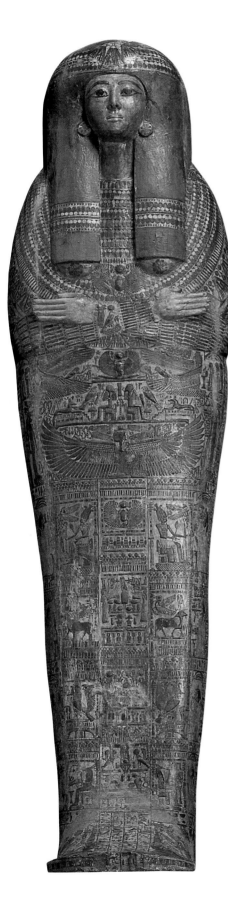

38 Coffin and coffin board of Tanakhtnettahat

Dynasty 21, 1075–945 BC
Wood, pigment
Coffin: L. 181.5 cm; w. 52 cm; d. 55.5 cm
Board: L. 170 cm; w. 36 cm; d. 9.5 cm
1999.1.17 A–D
Charlotte Lichirie Collection of Egyptian Art

This unusual coffin was made for the Lady Tanakhtnettahat, a chantress in the temple of the god Amun at Karnak. Women served in temples not as priests, but as chantresses, or singers, who presumably played instruments and recited hymns to the gods. Such women were usually of high rank, as this fine coffin indicates.

On the coffin lid, the lady Tanakhtnettahat is outfitted in a full wig adorned with her finest jewelry. A fillet of lotus flowers and petals encircles the top of her head, and round earrings peek out from beneath her wig. The lappets of the wig are gathered in beaded bands and overlay a shawl-like broad collar. A winged goddess is spread across the chest of the coffin, and below are twinned scenes of an enthroned Osiris receiving offerings from Tanakhtnettahat. Below this is a composition of Isis and Nephthys worshiping the fetish of Abydos, which is flanked by Tanakhtnettahat adoring a ram-headed deity. The pattern of a central panel of amuletic devices and gods and goddesses being

venerated by the coffin owner continues on the remainder of the body of the coffin. At the foot end, goddesses are shown mourning a mummified figure.

The vignettes delicately painted on the sides of the coffin depict mythological scenes drawn from the *Book of the Dead*. The images on the proper left side of the coffin begin at the foot end with a depiction of a pyramid-topped private tomb in the desert, guarded by Anubis and Hathor of Deir el-Bahri. Before this is a symbol of the goddess of the west and a scene of Tanakhtnettahat worshiping the tree goddess. The next panel depicts a divine barque being drawn through the heavens and adored by *ba*-birds. Tanakhtnettahat is then shown before two figures of Re enthroned in a kiosk, followed by an image of the god Thoth. The last scene shows the fetish of Abydos being praised by Nephthys and Isis, while Nephthys is depicted with wings outstretched at the head end of the coffin.

The scenes on the proper right side of the coffin show Osiris being praised by Nephthys and Isis. This is followed again by an image of Thoth and a composition with Nut, Shu, and Geb in their respective positions as emblems of the sky, air, and earth. Over the mummy was placed a coffin board, decorated in a manner quite similar to the lid, with a central band of winged scarabs and

Detail of goddess
painted on floor
of coffin bottom.

pectoral ornaments flanked by deities. It is uninscribed, but appears to have been executed by a hand similar to that of the coffin lid, suggesting it was part of the original assemblage.

A particularly interesting feature of this coffin is that it shows extensive reworking on both the interior and exterior. The mummy that was inside the coffin, although clearly of the period, was rather poorly preserved, and examination revealed that none of her internal organs had been removed. An examination of the text revealed that Tanakht-nettahat's names have been erased and, in one case, written over with the name of a woman named Ta-Aset.

In addition to the altered inscriptions, there were a number of areas of ancient overpainting and restoration. The most extensive reworking seems to have been on the image of the goddess of the west shown on the bottom of the coffin. This area seems to have been damaged, possibly by the removal of the mummy of

Tanakhtnettahat, and then parts covered over and repainted for the burial of Ta-Aset. The figures of the gods on the interior sides of the coffin have also been entirely painted over in red, and the only complete image that remains is that of Isis vanquishing a serpent, which appears at the head end. Although recycling of funerary material seems to have occurred in a number of burials from this period, this coffin shows unusually extensive alterations.

An additional piece to this puzzling coffin concerns fragments from an outer coffin of similar style inscribed for a chantress of Amun named Tanakhtnettahat, now in Grenoble. These may have been left from the original burial, since they do not evidence the same erasures of the name; the missing lid and broken condition of the latter may give further weight to this supposition.

39 Coffin and mummy of Pashedkhonsu

Dynasty 21, 1075–945 BC
Wood, pigment, linen, human remains
Coffin: L. 187.5 cm; w. 51.5 cm;
d. (at foot) 64 cm
Mummy: L. 170 cm; w. 38 cm
1999.1.15 A, B (coffin); 1999.1.16 (mummy)
Charlotte Lichirie Collection of Egyptian Art

Like many of the most beautiful coffins of the Twenty-first Dynasty, this one belonged to a high official from Thebes— Pashedkhonsu, high priest of Amun at Karnak. With the wealth and power of a de facto royal court centered at the great temple, the priests of Karnak had access to the finest goods for their own burials.

Pashedkhonsu is shown wearing the divine beard that associates him with Osiris, the god of the dead. His chest is covered with a representation of an elaborate floral collar, through which his clenched fists emerge. Scarabs and sacred images decorate the rest of the lid in designs modeled in plaster to give them a three-dimensional quality as if they were actual jewels. The shimmering, yellow varnish mimicked the sheen of gold, giving the entire piece the appearance of the most sumptuous of sepulchers.

The sides of the coffin are also elaborately decorated and show Pashedkhonsu seated and standing in front of piles of food offerings and various gods. Outside the head end of the coffin is a much-worn depiction of a *djed*-pillar and on the proper right is a representation of the goddess Hathor standing in a solar boat, being worshipped by a flock of ba-birds. This is followed by Pashedkhonsu standing before a heaped offering table and facing the three enthroned gods.

The other side is painted in a similar way, but with varying details. A ram-headed solar deity stands in the boat, and Pashedkhonsu is positioned before a slightly different mound of offerings in front of three enthroned gods with still more variant arrangements.

The interior of the coffin has been somewhat damaged but still retains images of a goddess with sun disk and cow horns at the bottom standing above a *djed*-pillar. The sides are also imperfectly preserved but are decorated with depictions of mummiform gods standing before sketchily drawn offering tables, as is standard for the period. The interior of the head end is adorned with a frontal depiction of a *ba*-bird flanked by parallel offering inscriptions.

40 Coffin face

Mid–Third Intermediate Period, 945–712 BC
Wood, pigment
H. 16 cm; w. 16 cm; d. 12.5 cm
1999.1.145
Charlotte Lichirie Collection of Egyptian Art

On many coffins of the Third Intermediate Period which were made out
of soft local woods, a finely carved face
of hard wood has been inserted into the
lid. This economical use of imported and
recycled cedar and ebony would allow
the most important aspect of the coffin—
the visage—to be rendered in a precise
and lasting way. This face is painted red
to equate the deceased with the sun god.

41 Fragments of the coffin of Neskashuti

Dynasty 25, 760–656 BC
Wood, pigment, gesso, linen
L. 180 cm; w. 54 cm; d. (at head) 42 cm
1999.1.9 A, B
Charlotte Lichirie Collection of Egyptian Art

This coffin belonged to a man named
Neskashuti, Chief of the singers of Min,
son of Paenmiw, Divine Father of Min,
and Overseer of the singers of Min.
Possibly made in Akhmim, the primary
cult center of Min, the coffin displays
a rather eccentric and unrefined style
typical of provincial artisans.

The broad facial features are typical
of coffins of the Twenty-fifth, or Nubian,
Dynasty, as is the sculptural design, with
back pillar and plinth below the feet.
The decoration relies heavily on inscriptions, and the bottom half is covered
with rows of text on alternating yellow
and white bands.

Neskashuti wears a heavy wig banded
by a fillet and a floral broad collar.
On the crown of the head, a figure of
a goddess supports a solar disk between
her upraised arms.

The representation of a goddess with
spread wings kneels on the chest. Below
her, a figure of the deceased worships
Osiris, who leads a procession of mummiform deities. The lower portion of
the body is divided by a column of text,
with detailed, polychrome glyphs, in contrast to the cursorily executed signs on
the rest of the coffin. Two columns of
mummiform gods are depicted on either
side of the central inscription. The horizontal orientation of the figures, along
with the fact that both columns are ori-
ented in the same direction, emphasizes
the provincial origin of the coffin.

On the front of the pedestal, the
mummy is portrayed on the lion-shaped
embalming bed with the Canopic jars
containing his viscera arranged below.
Ten mummiform deities and a priest
stand at either end of the bed. The bottom
of the pedestal shows a figure of the Apis
bull bearing the mummy on its back, as a
ba-bird hovers overhead. Although these

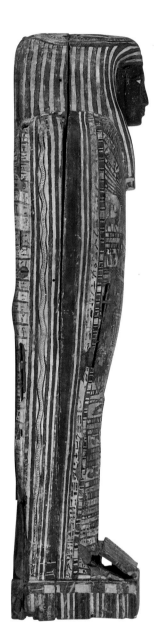

scenes are not uncommon on coffins of
this period, the rather rough execution
of certain figures, such as the *ba*-bird and
the Canopic jars, highlights the less rigid
artistic standards found outside of Thebes.

When this coffin arrived at the Carlos,
its lid was almost completely smashed,
and the pieces were heavily blackened
by grime and soot. Fragments were even
scattered among the other coffins in
the collection. Following a lengthy,
painstaking conservation effort, the
coffin of Neskashuti has regained its
original charm.

42 Inner and outer coffins of Iawttayesheret

Dynasty 25, 760–656 BC
Wood, gesso, pigment
Outer: L. 191 cm; w. 66 cm; d. (at foot) 66.5 cm
Inner: L. 171 cm; w. 52 cm; d. (at head) 42 cm
1999.1.8 A–D
Charlotte Lichirie Collection of Egyptian Art

This lovely nested set of coffins belonged to a woman named Iawttayesheret, also called Tayesheret. The daughter of Padikhnum and Tadiaset, Iawttayesheret was the great follower of the Divine Adoratrice of Amun, and almost certainly resided in Thebes. Both her titles and the high quality of her coffins indicate that Iawttayesheret was a woman of some stature.

The Nubian kings of the Twenty-fifth Dynasty reunited Egypt following the political upheaval of the Third Intermediate Period. In order to reinforce their rule, they installed female members of the royal family in the office of the Divine Adoratrice of Amun, the highest position in the temple of the national deity. These women enjoyed unprecedented power and independence and surrounded themselves with men and women of status and wealth. Iawttayesheret, the owner of this coffin, belonged to this elite group as one of the leaders of the retinue of the Divine Adoratrice.

In addition to restoring political order to Egypt, the Nubian kings instigated an artistic renaissance, evoking in particular the legacy of the Old Kingdom. Many members of the Theban aristocracy built enormous, skillfully decorated tombs around the temple of Hatshepsut at Deir el-Bahri, often containing scenes taken directly from earlier sources. Coffins for high-status burials during this period displayed a rather more austere style than those of the preceding Third Intermediate Period and adopted sculptural features such as a wide back pillar and pedestal. Nested sets of coffins continued to be used, although the outer case was typically of rectangular form, with a vaulted lid and posts at each corner.

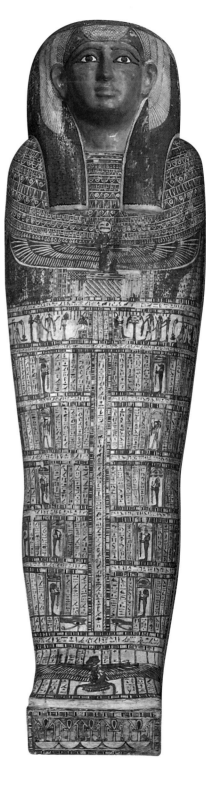

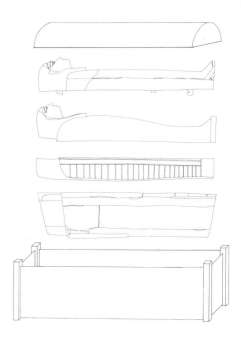

The decoration of the lid of the inner coffin typifies that of coffins of this period, with large sections of text broken up by figures and vignettes. Iawttayesheret wears a voluminous tripartite wig topped by a vulture headdress and encircled by a floral fillet. On the crown of her head, the goddess Nephthys stands with wings outstretched, surrounded by columns of text that invoke the goddess and list the name and titles of the deceased. A floral *wesekh* collar covers the chest above a kneeling figure of Nut, the sky goddess, who spreads her wings protectively

across the body. Below the goddess are back-to-back illustrations of the divine judgment. Each scene depicts the weighing of the heart, with the god Thoth recording the results as the demon Ammit anxiously waits below the scale. The other half of each scene shows Osiris enthroned before a laden offering table as Thoth and Ma'at, the goddess of truth, lead Iawttayesheret toward him.

The body of the inner lid is arranged into five registers separated by a line of text and divided by a central column of text requesting offerings on behalf of

the deceased. The panels on each side of the text column contain central figures flanked by three columns of text. The figures represent mummiform funerary deities and Anubis, the god of embalming. A depiction of the goddess Nephthys decorates the feet, which rest upon a pedestal. The bottom of the pedestal shows the sacred Apis bull, associated with Osiris, bearing the mummy of Iawttayesheret.

The case of the inner coffin is adorned exclusively with inscriptions, both inside and out. The bottom of the inside contains rows of text on alternating yellow and white backgrounds, with two lines of hieroglyphics running around the wall. With the exception of the wig, the outside of the base is also covered by rows of inscription. Many examples from this period depict the *djed*-pillar associated with Osiris on the back pillar of the coffin. In this instance, however, six columns of text fill that space.

The massive outer coffin is made of long planks with minimal embellishment, in order to highlight the surface of the wood. The wig, the floral broad collar, and a single column of text comprise the only decoration. As on the inner coffin, the wig is surmounted by a vulture headdress and fillet. A solar disk between a pair of crowned uraei appears on the crown of the head. The inscription records the name, titles, and filiation of the deceased. On the base of the coffin, there is no decoration other than a line of text around the circumference. In several places, mud plaster was applied to mask knots in the wood or joins between boards. The spare, elegant figure of the goddess of the west assumes her customary place on the bottom of the case.

It seems that Iawttayesheret owned a three-part nested set of coffins. In addition to the two cases at the Carlos, fragments of her outer coffin have been located at the Medelhausmuseet in Stockholm. The fragments are from a cornerpost of the outermost coffin, indicating that it was of the vaulted, rectangular variety popular during the Twenty-fifth Dynasty.

43 Coffin and mummy of a child

Dynasties 25–26, 760–525 BC
Coniferous wood, pigment, gesso, human remains, linen
Coffin: L. 130 cm; w. 45 cm; d. (at foot) 48 cm
Mummy: L. 56 cm; w., 20 cm; d. 16 cm
1999.1.6 A, B (coffin); 1999.1.1 (mummy)
Charlotte Lichirie Collection of Egyptian Art

This finely crafted coffin contains the mummy of a child, approximately two years of age. Although the cause of death cannot be determined, this mummy does have one very interesting feature, or lack thereof: the legs of the mummy are missing just below the knees, and the absence of any signs of healing suggests that the damage was postmortem.

The sparse, simple ornamentation of the coffin highlights the beautifully grained wood. Only the face, wig, and floral collar are painted, with a single column of text running the length of the coffin. The heavy features and broad face are characteristic of the Twenty-

fifth, or Nubian, Dynasty, though the minimal decoration suggests that this coffin may have come from the Twenty-sixth Dynasty. The elegant figure painted inside the base represents one of the goddesses charged with protecting the deceased—perhaps Nut, Hathor, or the goddess of the west. The preparation of the mummy offers further evidence of a date in the Twenty-fifth or Twenty-sixth Dynasty. The wide band of red linen vertically encircling the mummy is a distinctive feature of wrappings during this period. In many cases, the mummy was completely covered by a red shroud

or a sheet with red borders.

The truncated proportions of the coffin, along with the rarity of coffins constructed specifically for children, suggest that the child within was not the intended occupant. The bottom of the coffin was cut off and a new foot added in a rather makeshift manner, effectively "downsizing" the coffin for a child. The inscription, identifying the owner and requesting offerings for his sustenance in the afterlife, was clearly added after the coffin was reworked, since it extends onto the replacement foot.

High mortality rates among infants and children in ancient Egypt meant that few families were financially able to provide a coffin for every child they buried. This fact, combined with the quality of the coffin, indicate that the deceased, a boy named Hori, belonged to a family of some status.

44 Late Dynastic coffin

Dynasties 27–30, 525–343 BC
Wood, plaster, pigment
L. 182 cm; w. 45 cm; d. 35.2 cm
1921.3 A, B
Collected by William A. Shelton,
funded by John A. Manget

The angular, unpolished appearance of
this coffin attests to the decline in quality
of burial equipment during the later
stages of Egyptian rule. The crude, unso-
phisticated decoration of this piece suggest that it was produced by a provincial
artisan, rather than a high-status atelier.

The goddess of the west appears on
the bottom of the base, identified by
the falcon standard upon her head,
which represents the hieroglyph meaning
"west." The Egyptians associated the
west, where the sun sets each evening,
with the entrance to the underworld.
The goddess guarded the necropolis and
the dead during the dangerous transition
to the afterlife.

On the lid, the divine wig and beard
identify the deceased with Osiris, the
god of the underworld who was killed
by his brother Seth and subsequently
resurrected. Despite its rough execution,
the decoration of the coffin retains
traditional motifs such as the goddess
spreading her wings protectively across
the body, and the mummy on the lion-
shaped embalming bed. The Canopic
jars, which would hold the mummified
organs of the deceased, appear below
the bed. The lids of the jars represent
the four sons of Horus, who are also
portrayed with mummiform bodies
on the lower portion of the coffin.

Five columns of roughly executed
text run down the center of the lid. The
three central columns contain a standard
formula requesting offerings for the sustenance of the deceased in the afterlife.
Unfortunately, damage has obliterated
the name of the deceased. The two outer
columns identify the flanking images
of the four sons of Horus.

45 Mummy with cartonnage trappings

Late Ptolemaic Period, 167–30 BC
Human remains, linen, cartonnage, pigment, gilt
L. 170 cm; w. 43.5 cm; d. 25.4 cm
1921.6
Collected by William A. Shelton,
funded by John A. Manget

The start of the Ptolemaic Period witnessed a change in both the form and decoration of funerary equipment. The production of decorated anthropoid coffins declined even as the wrapping and embellishment of mummies became more elaborate. The inner coffins and mummy boards found in previous periods were replaced by trappings made of cartonnage. Consisting of layers of linen soaked with an adhesive and thinly coated with plaster, cartonnage was an inexpensive, easily manufactured alternative to wood. Ptolemaic mummies were typically equipped with a helmet-style mask, a boot for the feet, and several panels along the body that were fastened to the shroud.

The mummy shown here, that of a middle-aged man, wears a mask with gilded face, identifying him with the sun god. The chest is covered by one panel in the shape of a broad collar and another depicting a winged scarab and Nut, the goddess of the sky, who spreads her wings protectively across the body. The plaque atop the legs shows the mummy resting on a lion bed, with the goddesses Isis and Nephthys mourning at either end, just as they did for their brother Osiris, god of the dead. The foot case is adorned with figures of Anubis, the god of embalming, in the form of a reclining jackal. Rows of rearing cobras crowned with solar disks appear in place of the toes.

A single column of text, a standard offering formula, runs the length of the leg panel and foot case. Unfortunately, the name of the deceased is not included. Cartonnage trappings were frequently fabricated quickly or even purchased ready-made, with carelessly executed texts that omit details such as the name of the individual.

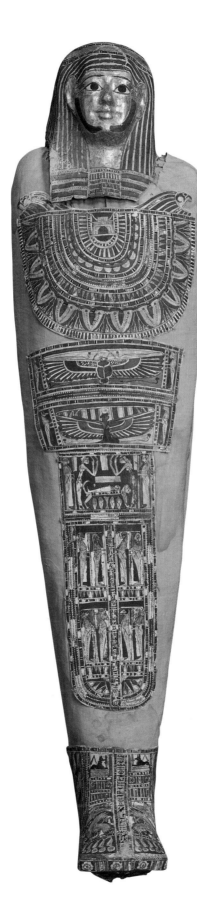

46 Cartonnage mask

Roman, Fourth century AD
Linen, plaster, pigment
H. 18 cm; w. 16 cm; d. 6 cm
1999.1.143
Charlotte Lichirie Collection of Egyptian Art

In the later Roman period, mummies were no longer placed in decorated anthropoid coffins but were merely covered with painted shrouds. The face of the shroud was made of plaster, molded into a three-dimensional mask, with details of the upper torso rendered below in two dimensions. Two groups of mummies adorned in this manner were discovered at Deir el-Bahri, the first by Edouard Naville in 1895 and the second by H. E. Winlock in 1924.

The mask shown here is typical of the late Roman funerary style found in and around Thebes, with its theatrically painted details. The staring, heavily rimmed eyes, curling lashes, and hair modeled in plaster all characterize the masks that Winlock uncharitably described as "atrocities of hideousness."[1]

1. H. E. Winlock, *Excavations at Deir El Bahri: 1911–1931* (New York, 1942), 99.

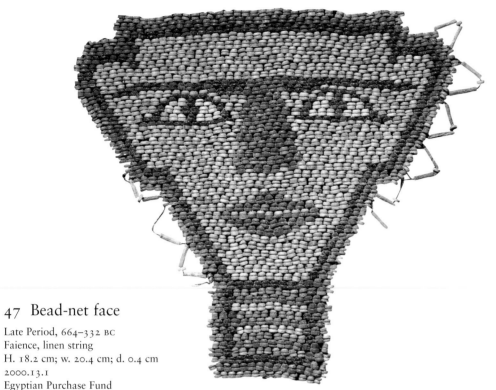

47 Bead-net face

Late Period, 664–332 BC
Faience, linen string
H. 18.2 cm; w. 20.4 cm; d. 0.4 cm
2000.13.1
Egyptian Purchase Fund

A feature of Late Period burials was the covering of the mummy with a network composed of faience beads. This first appeared in the Third Intermediate Period, although beadwork garments were used for burials in the Old and Middle Kingdoms.

The bead-networks of the Late Period are thought to derive from the costumes worn by goddesses, although they have been found on mummies of both sexes. When they initially appeared, they served as a simple covering over the body, with winged scarabs and images of the four sons of Horus worked in. By the Late Period they expanded to include occasional bands of text and a face mask, all done in painstaking patterns of tiny colored faience beads.

48 Winged scarab

Dynasty 25 or later, after 760 BC
Faience
H. 3.4 cm; w. 9.9 cm; d. 0.3 cm
1921.66 A
Collected by William A. Shelton,
funded by John A. Manget

The powerful regenerative symbolism of the scarab accounts for its popularity as a funerary amulet. Large winged scarabs were sewn onto mummy wrappings or incorporated into bead-net shrouds. These compositions could be made out of faience or beadwork, as in this example.

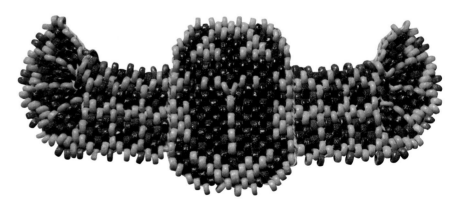

AMULETS AND FUNERARY JEWELRY

49 Scarab

Late–Ptolemaic Periods, 664–30 BC
Gold
L. 2.8 cm; w. 1.8 cm
1921.192
Collected by William A. Shelton,
funded by John A. Manget

The scarab beetle was a symbol of
resurrection and rebirth, and amulets
in its image were frequently placed on
the mummy near the heart. The beetle
hieroglyph represents the word meaning
"to come into being," indicating its
potency. Amulets were often mass-produced in the Late Period by hammering
sheet gold into stone molds, which
is how this piece was manufactured.

50 Funerary amulets

Late Period, 664–332 BC
Obsidian
Collected by William A. Shelton,
funded by John A. Manget

A. Heart amulet
1921.72
H. 2.6 cm; w. 1.4 cm; d. 0.8 cm

B. Isis knot (tyet)
1921.81
H. 4.1 cm; w. 1.4 cm; d. 0.4 cm

C. *Djed*-pillar
1921.79
H. 4.6 cm; w. 1.6 cm; d. 0.4 cm

D. Two fingers amulet
1921.75
H. 6.3 cm; w. 2.2 cm; d. 0.5 cm

These are some of the amulets that
would be found on a single mummy.
The shape, color, and location of each
amulet on the body indicated its ritual
importance. Amulets were usually placed
according to their different magical
functions. For example, the heart amulet
rested over the heart and the *djed*-pillar
lay on the spine.

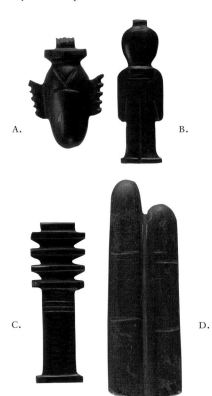

A.

B.

C.

D.

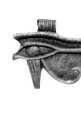

51 *Wedjat* eye mold and amulet

New Kingdom or later, after 1539 BC
Faience, ceramic
Mold: Diam. 4.3 cm
Amulet: L. 0.5 cm; w. 0.6 cm
1921.11 (mold)
Collected by William A. Shelton,
funded by John A. Manget
2001.10.1 (amulet)
Anonymous gift

Amulets in faience were produced in
great multiples for burials. The faience
was formed in open-faced pottery molds
and, when dry, removed and fired. The
transformation of the powdery white
raw material into the glistening, bright
blue faience must have made the charm
seem even more magical.

The *wedjat* eye, or the eye of Horus,
was one of the most potent of all
Egyptian symbols. It represents the eye
of the falcon-headed god who lost it
fighting to avenge the death of his father,
Osiris. According to myth, the eye was
magically healed by the god Thoth, and
so came to be associated with miraculous
restorative power.

52 *Menat* (necklace counterweight) amulet

New Kingdom, 1539–1075 BC
Faience
H. 2.3 cm; w. 0.9 cm; d. 0.5 cm
L1998.62.87
Promised gift

Counterweights, originally worn to
keep heavy necklaces in place, eventually
became more decorative than the necklaces themselves. They could also be
rendered in miniature as amulets, as
in this example. Associated with the
goddess Hathor, they were often given
by her priestesses to the deceased.

53 Seal amulet of Isis and Horus

First Intermediate Period, 2130–1980 BC
Steatite
H. 1.8 cm; w. 0.5 cm; d. 0.5 cm
2000.9.1
Gift of Dr. Jerome Eisenberg

Seal amulets appear quite early as tomb
offerings and could either be actual
name seals used in life or merely symbolic
tokens. This seal represents an unusual
double image of the child-god Horus
on the lap of his mother, Isis.

Twinned motifs such as this appear
on seals of the First Intermediate Period,
and this maternal image is appropriate,
since the majority of these seals are
found in the graves of women and
children. The carvings on the underside
of the seal are not hieroglyphic symbols,
but random shapes, indicating that
this was probably not a functional seal.
During this disruption of the First Intermediate Period, literacy seems to have
suffered with the breakdown of the cen-
tralized state, leading to the manufacture
of items with pseudo-hieroglyphs.

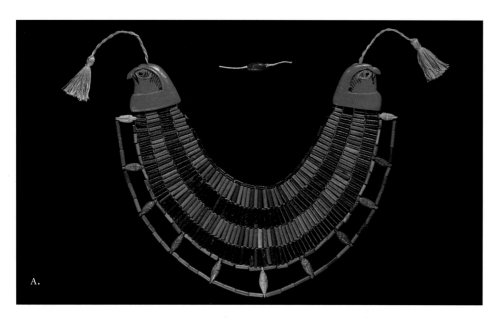

A.

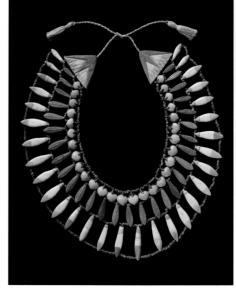

54 Middle Kingdom broad collar and scarabs

Dynasty 12, 1938–1759 BC
Promised gifts

A. Broad Collar
2001.15.1
H. (max.) 21 cm; w. (max.) 25.5 cm
Faience, modern reconstruction

B. Amethyst scarab
L1998.62.124 B
L. 2 cm; w. 1.3 cm

C. Carnelian scarab
L1998.62.124 A
L. 2 cm; w. 1.3 cm

D. Jasper scarab
L1998.62.124 C
L. 1.3 cm; w. 1 cm

B.

C.

D.

Sets of jewelry in beautiful colors were a recurring feature in Middle Kingdom burials. Of particular significance was the *sweret* bead, a barrel shaped bead, usually made of carnelian and worn on a string around the neck, which was believed to protect the throat.

The beaded broad collar with the falcon terminals was specified as part of the funerary equipment needed by the deceased in the coffin texts. The association with the god Horus undoubtedly gave this piece of jewelry magical healing quality.

Scarabs also become frequent objects of adornment in this period and are worn either as rings with simple string or wire shanks, or as part of necklaces. The scarab which lays its eggs in a ball of dung and then emerges from it represented spontaneous generation to the Egyptians and as such had powerful re-birth symbolism.

55 Reconstructed broad collar

New Kingdom, 1539–1075 BC
Faience, modern reconstruction
L. 45 cm; w. 8 cm
2001.9.1
Gift of Yvonne Markowitz

Apart from serving as items of adornment, jewelry had powerful amuletic properties for both the living and the dead. The invention of polychrome faience with a wide variety of subtle hues in the late Eighteenth Dynasty allowed the production of collars imitating garlands of fruit and flowers. Such ornaments made from vegetal material sewn onto papyrus backing were an important part of the funerary ceremony and were known as *wah*-collars.

These collars are represented on coffins as well as on other funerary offerings, and actual examples made of flower petals, fruit and plant material, or faience simulations were included in the tomb and could be placed on the mummy. The symbolism extended beyond the collar itself to the various elements that composed it. The blue lotus flower terminals and pendant petals on this example symbolized rebirth, and the mandrake fruits and palm leaves, fertility.

56 Funerary jewelry

New Kingdom, 1539–1075 BC

A. Fillet
Faience
1999.1.123
H. 4 cm; l. 13 cm
Charlotte Lichirie Collection of Egyptian Art

B. Ear spool
Faience
Diam. 4.5 cm
L1998.62.103
Promised gift

C. Snake head amulet
Carnelian
L. 1.7 cm; w. 1 cm
L1998.62.107
Promised gift

D. Heart amulet
Glass
L. 1 cm
L1998.62.85
Promised gift

E. Bracelet spacer
Faience
L. 4.5 cm; w. 2.8 cm
L1998.62.99
Promised gift

F. *Wedjat*-eye ring
Faience
L. 2 cm; w. 2 cm
2000.14.1
Gift in memory of James Robins

G. Scarab
Faience
L. 1.9 cm; w. 1 cm
L1998.62.122 A
Promised gift

The wealth of a far-flung empire flowing into the country in the New Kingdom manifested itself in the luxurious fashions worn by the Egyptians. Men and women, living and dead, were bedizened with jewelry from head to foot. Many items of adornment had floral symbols of rejuvenation and rebirth, particularly the lotus. Beaded fillets could be worn on the head by both sexes, and earrings, introduced from Nubia, were worn by both men and women.

Amulets such as the carnelian serpent head were thought to protect from all manner of ills—in this case, snakebite. Even bracelets could be combined with amuletic motifs and symbols. Rings were made of stone, metal, or faience, and could be worn on every finger. They could also serve as settings for scarabs, which could again be both ornamental and symbolic.

ANIMAL MUMMIES AND CULTS

57 Falcon mummy

Late Period, 664–332 BC
Linen, animal remains
H. 38.1 cm; w. 11.7 cm; diam. 7.7 cm
1958.63
Collection of Dr. J. Philips

This falcon mummy is covered with an intricate pattern of wrappings done in natural and dyed brown linen. The details of the face and head of the bird have been rendered in paint over a white gesso ground.

The falcon was identified from the earliest times with the sun god Horus and the reigning king, who was his manifestation on earth. The raptor was also associated with a number of other gods, including Re-Horakhty, Sokar, Montu, and various regional forms of Horus. Deposits of falcon mummies have been found at Buto, Giza, Saqqara, Abydos, and Kom Ombo.

Animal Mummies
Many species of animals were mummified in the later periods of Egyptian history. These were not pets, but sacred animals that were raised in temple precincts. The animals were sacrificed, mummified almost as elaborately as humans, and offered in the temples by pious pilgrims as a substitute for more expensive bronze votives. When a sufficient number had collected in the temple, the animal mummies would be buried by the priests in sacred animal cemeteries. Included were cats and dogs, ibises and falcons, and even fish, snakes, and shrews.

58 Ibis mummy

Late period, 664–332 BC
Linen, animal remains
H. 29 cm; w. 11 cm
1999.1.24
Charlotte Lichirie Collection of Egyptian Art

The sacred ibis is an African wading bird related to the heron, with a distinctive long, curving yellow bill and white and black plumage. It is no longer found in Egypt, but vast cemeteries of ibis mummies have been found throughout Egypt. The ibis was associated with Thoth, the god of wisdom and learning, and large numbers of ibis mummies were found at Hermopolis, his main cult center. Many such votives were elaborately wrapped or placed in decorated coffins, sometimes made in the shape of an ibis. Less costly versions such as this example were simply wrapped in linen.

59 Cat mummy

Late Period, 664–332 G.
Linen, animal remains
H. 30 cm; w. 9 cm
1999.1.25
Charlotte Lichirie Collection of Egyptian Art

Cats were associated with the goddess Bastet and revered as protectors of the home. Great quantities of mummies of cats were left at cult centers of the goddess at Saqqara and other cult sites in the Delta and Middle Egypt.

X-rays reveal that this example is actually a simulated mummy with a cat skull and a stray bone forming the body. It has been wrapped and detailed in paint to look like a complete cat mummy. Such simulated mummies were not uncommon, given the vast amounts of animals that were buried. Many animal burials seem to have occurred at a single time, perhaps during festivals. If there were not enough actual creatures around to be offered, then substitutes had to be produced.

60 Figure of a cat

Dynasty 26, 664—525 BC
Bronze
H. 7 cm; w. 2 cm; d. 4.5 cm
1999.1.43
Charlotte Lichirie Collection of Egyptian Art

The cat was honored throughout Egyptian history as both a pet and a domestic guardian, keeping the household free of pests. In addition, the cat was associated with the goddess Bastet, who often appears with a human body and feline head. The primary cult center of Bastet was located at Bubastis (modern Tell Basta), where enormous numbers of mummified cats have been discovered within the temple precinct.

In the Late Period and thereafter, sacred animals were bred, mummified, and presented as offerings in temples before being buried in special necropoleis. The coffins for these mummies took two forms: a narrow box with a figure of the animal on the lid or a box in the shape of the animal itself. This diminutive example is not large enough to hold even a kitten and probably sat atop a small wood or bronze coffin. Tangs for attaching the figure to the box are preserved below the front paws and the tail.

61 Falcon figure

Late Period, 664–332 BC
Bronze
H. 20 cm; w. 6.5 cm; d. 15 cm
1999.1.49
Charlotte Lichirie Collection of Egyptian Art

This image of a falcon could have adorned the casket of a mummified bird. Mummies of falcons and other birds were placed in bronze boxes surmounted by an image of a falcon and left as offerings in temples and sacred sites.

62 Votives for Apis

A. Stela dedicated to the Apis bull

Dynasties 19–20, 1279–1075 BC
Limestone
H. 16.3 cm; w. 11.6 cm
X.2.41
Collected by William A. Shelton,
funded by John A. Manget

B. Shabti for the Apis bull

Late Period, 664–332 BC
Faience
H. 9.6 cm; w. 4.8 cm
L1999.37
Promised gift

C. Figure of the Apis bull

Dynasty 26, 664–525 BC
Bronze
H. 7.5 cm; w. 5 cm; l. 7 cm
1999.1.42
Charlotte Lichirie Collection of Egyptian Art

Although there is evidence of cults dedicated to animals as early as the Predynastic Period, their popularity did not peak until the Late Ptolemaic Periods. Animals sacred to certain deities were bred, sacrificed, mummified, and buried in huge necropoleis within the temple precincts. The cult of the Apis bull was one of the oldest animal cults and ultimately, the most renowned. Unlike other cults that might sacrifice thousands of animals, that of the Apis bull centered around a single, chosen animal.

A fertility god called Apis was venerated as early as the First Dynasty, although the deity ultimately merged with Ptah, a creator-god. The Apis bull was considered the physical manifestation of Ptah, containing the ba, or essence, of the deity. Worshipped in the cult center of Ptah at Memphis, the Apis was treated to a coronation ceremony and a luxurious lifestyle in a sacred precinct. Each bull

was selected after an exhaustive search throughout Egypt. According to Herodotus, the fifth-century BC Greek historian, the Apis bull "is the calf of a cow which is never afterwards able to have another. …a flash of light descends upon the cow from heaven, and this causes her to receive Apis. The Apis-calf has distinctive marks: it is black, with a white diamond on its forehead, the image of an eagle on its back, the hairs on its tail double, and a scarab under its tongue" (Book 3, ch. 29).

The death of the Apis bull was accompanied by even greater ceremony than its installation. Beginning in the reign of Amenhotep III, the bull was mummified just as a human would have been and entombed in an enormous sarcophagus in a necropolis known as the Serapeum. Located at Saqqara, the Serapeum was actively used for Apis burials from the New Kingdom until the Ptolemaic Period. Just as with a human

A.

B.

burial, the Apis was provided with extensive funerary equipment, including Canopic jars and shabtis, both of which were typically bull-headed. The Apis bull and the Serapeum were the focus of intense public piety beginning in the Late Period. Within the subterranean chambers and corridors of the Serapeum, hundreds of visitors dedicated stelae and votive images of the bull as signs of their devotion. Small, bronze figures were particularly popular, often depicting the donor kneeling before the Apis, or simply the bull with an inscription. Stelae of all sizes and levels of quality were inserted in the walls throughout the Serapeum, typically portraying the dedicant paying homage to Apis. In this instance, several donors appear before the crowned bull, including both men and women, probably members of the same family.

Upon its death, the Apis bull was identified with Osiris in a syncretized form known as Osiris-Apis or Osorapis.

Ptolemy I Soter (ca. 305–285 BC) introduced a cult specifically devoted to this deity in a Hellenized form as Serapis. The cult of Serapis, in conjunction with that of Isis, the wife of Osiris manifest in the mother of the Apis bull, was wholeheartedly embraced by the Graeco-Roman world, spreading to its farthest boundaries. The Apis bull represented one of the most enduring aspects of Egyptian religion and culture, venerated until the destruction of the Serapeum in the fourth century AD, when the Emperor Honorius banned the use of pagan sanctuaries.

C.

Bibliography

Arnold, Dorothea. *An Egyptian Bestiary.* New York, 1995.

Baines, John, and Peter Lacovara. "Death, the Dead, and Burial in Ancient Egyptian Society." *Journal of Social Archaeology* (forthcoming).

Brech-Neldner, Ruth. *Der Mumiensarkophag des Nes-pa-kai-schuti.* Detmold, 1992.

D'Auria, Sue, Peter Lacovara, and Catharine Roehrig. *Mummies and Magic: The Funerary Arts of Ancient Egypt.* Boston, 1988.

Douglas, James, Jr. *Honeymoon on the Nile.* 1861.

Faulkner, Raymond. *The Egyptian Book of the Dead: The Book of Going Forth by Day.* San Francisco, 1994.

Graefe, Erhart. *Untersuchungen zur Verwaltung und Geschichte der Institution der Gottesgemahlin des Amun vom Beginn des neuen Reiches bis zur Spätzeit.* Wiesbaden, 1981.

Grenoble Musée des Beaux-Arts. *Collection Égyptienne.* Paris, 1979.

Harris, James E., and Kent R. Weeks. *X-Raying the Pharaohs.* New York, 1973.

Ikram, Salima, and Aidan Dodson. *The Mummy in Ancient Egypt: Equipping the Dead for Eternity.* London, 1998.

Kitchen, Kenneth A. *The Third Intermediate Period in Egypt (1100–650 BC).* Warminster, 1986.

Michael C. Carlos Museum. *Handbook.* Atlanta, 1996.

Museum of Fine Arts, Boston. *Egypt's Golden Age: The Art of Living in the New Kingdom 1558–1085 BC.* Boston, 1982.

Niwinski, Andrzej. *21st Dynasty Coffins from Thebes.* Mainz, 1988.

———. *Studies on the Illustrated Theban Funerary Papyri of the 11th and 10th Centuries BC.* Freiburg, 1989.

Ranke, Hermann. *Die ägyptischen Personennamen.* 2 vols. Glückstadt, 1935–52.

Robins, Gay. *The Art of Ancient Egypt.* Cambridge, 1997.

———. *Monuments and Mummies: The Shelton Expedition to Egypt.* Atlanta, 1989.

Shelton, William A. *Dust and Ashes of Empires.* Atlanta, 1922.

Stewart, Harry M. *Egyptian Shabtis.* Buckinghamshire, 1995.

Taylor, John H. *Death and the Afterlife in Ancient Egypt.* Chicago, 2001.

———. *Egyptian Coffins.* Aylesbury, 1989.

Trigger, Bruce G., et al. *Ancient Egypt: A Social History.* Cambridge, 1983.

Winlock, H. E. *Excavations at Deir el Bahri 1911–1931.* New York, 1942.

Index